UNLOCKING DESTINIES FROM THE COURTS OF HEAVEN

DISSOLVING CURSES THAT DELAY AND DENY OUR FUTURE

ROBERT HENDERSON

DEDICATION

This book is dedicated to all the saints in heaven and earth who together operate in the Courts of Heaven. Their activity together with all other heavenly dimensions secure God's will in the earth.

May we be counted worthy of the sacrifice of the Lord Jesus Christ and the sacrifice of those who laid down their lives for His Kingdom's will. Let His grace empower us to serve Him with reverence and godly fear.

CONTENTS

PREFACE

This book is a follow up to my book *Operating In The Courts Of Heaven: Granting God The Legal Right To Fulfill His Passion And Answer Our Prayer*. In this second volume of the *Operating In The Courts of Heaven* series, I talk about how to unlock the destinies of our lives and even nations from the legal dimension of the Spirit. I would strongly urge the first book in this series to be read as well as this one. Reading the first book will definitely help in understanding this one fully.

Each one of us has a book in Heaven with our destiny and purpose recorded in it. (Psalm 139:16) This book in Heaven is the reason we were created and exist in the earth. It is the Lord's passion to see us fulfill this destiny. The problem is our archenemy, the devil, also passionately desires to keep us from that destiny. If he can keep us out of our destiny, he can stop the purposes of God in the earth.

Our destiny and God's purposes are irrevocably joined. One of his chief weapons to do this is the landing and operation of curses. In the next pages, we will discover what some of these curses are and how to remove them from our lives. When this is done freedom will come for us to walk into the futures God has planned for us. Frustration carried for even the duration of our lives will end and satisfaction in life and living will be realized.

Remember, God has a plan that is full of good things for you. Jeremiah, chapter 29 and verse 11, declares the good intentions of God for your life.

> For I know the thoughts that I think toward you,
> says the LORD, thoughts of peace and not of evil,
> to give you a future and a hope. (Jeremiah 29:11)

Get ready for the future God has written in the books of Heaven for you. You can and will love life and see good days as curses are dissolved and destinies are apprehended. (1 Peter 3:10).

CHAPTER 1

CURSES ARE REAL

Curses are very real things. For many people when they hear the word curse, they think of a fairytale. Perhaps they think about a prince being turned into a frog through the incantation of a witch. Maybe their mind goes to a television show or movie where through black magic or white magic a spell is placed on someone or something. It could be that our minds return to a childhood time when a story was read to us of witchcraft in action. There are various ideas that accompany the word "curse."

The problem with these that I have mentioned and others is that it can make us think curses are fictitious in nature. Nothing can be further from the truth. Curses are real. If we do not realize this, we can be living under a curse and not know it. We have accepted the problems in our life as normal, not realizing they could have a spiritual root. This poses a problem. You cannot get free from something you don't know is there. The Lord wants us free to enjoy and experience the life we were created to live. The devil wants to steal it away. John, chapter 10, verse 10, tells us the passion of the Lord for us.

The thief does not come except to steal, and to kill, and to destroy. I have come that they may have life, and that they may have it more abundantly. (John 10:10)

The devil's purpose as "the thief" is to steal, kill and destroy. Jesus said that He, on the other hand, has come that we might have life and have it more abundantly. We have a God ordained destiny that we were built and fashioned for. We struggle to get into this destiny so often. Psalm, chapter 139, verse 16, tells us there is a book in Heaven that contains the destiny planned for us.

Your eyes saw my substance, being yet unformed. And in Your book they all were written, The days fashioned for me, When as yet there were none of them. (Psalm 139:16)

My substance or DNA was written in this book. In other words, what makes me tick. What resonates on the inside of me is determined by what was written in my book before time began. The things I am interested in, gifted in and gravitate towards were determined and written in my book. Plus, my days, which means how long I live and what my Kingdom purpose is during that time period were written in my book.

The problem is most people are frustrated because they

intuitively know they were created for more than what they have experienced. They know more is in their book than they have seen happen. The primary reason for this is curses against us that are denying and delaying our futures. We are being stolen from and need to know how to go into the Courts of Heaven and unlock our destinies by dissolving curses against us.

Some of the things the devil uses to steal our God-ordained life are these curses. My definition for a curse is "a spiritual force used by the devil to sabotage success and futures." When a curse is operating people are filled with frustrations because they can never quite reach what they intuitively know they were created for. They can't understand why things never seem to work for them. Even when everything is in place, the future they desire and long for will always seem to fall through and not happen. These people suffer from what the Bible calls "hope deferred." Proverbs, chapter 13, verse 12, tells us the effect of disappointment after disappointment in a person's life.

Hope deferred makes the heart sick, But when the desire comes, it is a tree of life. (Proverbs 13:12)

When people experience the dashing of their hope, dreams and desires over and over again it creates within them the inability to dream. To dream of the future becomes too painful. The pain of another disappointment is too much to go through. They have a sick heart. It is safer and less risky to just settle down in a life of existence, rather than believing God for something good, only to see it fail again. This can be the end result of a curse and/or curses operating. The answer is not to stop dreaming. The answer is to get the curse removed and their powers broken so dreams are not sabotaged and can come true. Life without dreams is not worth living. We were built by God to dream.

In my last book, *Operating In The Courts Of Heaven*, I explained that everything is legal in the spirit realm. The key to dealing with adverse forces that resist and work against us is to remove their legal rights. Curses can only operate from a legal position. Proverbs, chapter 26, verse 2, gives us some insight into the operation of curses.

> Like a flitting sparrow, like a flying swallow, So a curse without cause shall not alight. (Proverbs 26:2)

A curse has to have a cause or a legal right to land. The idea here is if our eyes were open to the spirit realm we would see curses flying around looking for a place to land. They cannot land just anywhere. They have to find a cause or legal reason to put their feet down. They are like flitting sparrows and flying swallows, looking for this legal place to land in our lives. This is why the Bible says that Satan is our adversary, "seeking" whom he may devour in 1 Peter, chapter 5, verse 8.

Be sober, be vigilant; because your adversary
the devil walks about like a roaring lion, seeking
whom he may devour. (1 Peter 5:8)

The word *adversary* is the Greek word *antidikos*, and
it means an opponent in a lawsuit. *Antidikos* comes from two
words, *anti* which means against something and *dikos* which
means rights. Our adversary or *antidikos* is one who is standing
against us, denying us what is rightfully ours. He uses the
legality of the spirit realm to bring curses on us. He does this to
stop us from obtaining all Jesus died for us to have.

So Satan is our legal foe who is bringing legal action
against us. He "seeks" a legal right to devour. If he discovers
one, then a curse can land because it now has a cause. To be
able to undo or remove a curse and stop its power against us we
must remove the legal reason it has found to land and operate.

The purpose of this book is to teach us how to go into
the Courts of Heaven and get things legally in place so every
curse is dissolved. When this occurs the limitations imposed by
the devil legally are removed. The key to undoing curses is to
recognize they are a legal issue and not a warfare issue. In other
words, we must go to court and not battle to dissolve curses.
The conflict we are in is a real one. It is just in the judicial
system of the spirit realm and not first on a battlefield. I cover
this extensively in *Operating In The Courts Of Heaven*.

Another crucial issue to dissolving curses is to recognize

they can operate among a New Testament people. I meet many people who think that if you have prayed a prayer to be born again then it is impossible for you to be cursed. They quote scriptures like Galatians, chapter 3, verse 13.

> Christ has redeemed us from the curse of the law, having become a curse for us (for it is written, "Cursed is everyone who hangs on a tree") (Galatians 3:13)

I want to be very clear. I believe that when Jesus provided His atoning work on the cross and was raised again and ascended to His place at the right hand of the Father that He dealt with every curse ... legally! When Jesus declared, "It is finished" on the cross, He was declaring that every legal requirement had been met for the reconciliation and reclaiming of all things back to God.

The problem is that it is one thing for a legal verdict to be rendered and another for the execution of it to take place. When a judge sits on a bench and renders a verdict, he doesn't then come down from that bench and enforce it. There are others who must take the legal rendering of the judge and execute it into place until it has practical and functional ramifications. Agencies, policemen and officers sent and recognized by the court have this job. If there is no one to do this, the verdict has no power functionally, even though legally it has been rendered.

This is best described by a happening with a young man that I know. This young man went through a very painful divorce. He didn't want the divorce, but was powerless to stop it. He had a two-year old little girl from this marriage that he loved dearly. After the divorce decree was issued and the divorce was final, this young man came to pick his little girl up for a holiday. The mother of the child, the young man's ex-wife, refused to give him his daughter. The young man was left no option other than to call the police.

When the police arrived they informed the young man that they did not go into homes and take a child from one parent to give to another parent. Even though he had a legal right to her, this was not something they would do. Of course this is understandable and right. The police explained to the young man that he would have to go to another governmental authority to enforce the divorce decree. The young man then asked the police who this governmental agency was. The police then made an astounding statement. They informed the young man that there was NO AGENCY to enforce divorce decrees. Wow!!

So even though the divorce decree was a legal verdict, it had NO FUNCTIONAL POWER because there were none to enforce it or execute it into place. This is exactly the situation in the spirit realm. Jesus Christ's death, burial and resurrection have allowed a verdict to be rendered. But as with a natural verdict it has to be executed into place for it to have functional power.

To fully see this principle, we should be aware of John, chapter 16, verses 8-11.

> And when He has come, He will convict the world of sin, and of righteousness, and of judgment: of sin, because they do not believe in Me; of righteousness, because I go to My Father and you see Me no more; of judgment, because the ruler of this world is judged. (John 16:8-11)

Jesus said when Holy Spirit would come, He would convict and convince us of sin, righteousness and judgment. The sin is one of unbelief. The Holy Spirit wars against our unbelief and seeks to bring us to realms of faith. He is committed to this process of being the "Author and Finisher" of our faith. (Hebrews 12: 2) The Holy Spirit also convinces us of what real righteousness is.

Jesus said the Spirit would do this because He was leaving and going to the Father. In other words, Jesus had displayed what real righteousness was, but would not be here to do this anymore. The Spirit would take His place and show us the right ways to live to please the Father. The Spirit would keep us out of the ditches of lawlessness and legalism. Without the Spirit helping us to understand real righteousness, we will get off the path of the Lord and into these ditches. Both bring death. We need Holy Spirit to guide us into all truth.

The other thing Jesus said the Spirit would do was convince us of judgment because the ruler of the world IS judged. Jesus was speaking as if He had already gone to the cross. He was saying the Holy Spirit would bring us the power and ability to execute into place the judgment of the cross. The ruler of this world, or the devil, was judged at the cross. The Holy Spirit came to empower us to be the officers of the court to execute into place that judgment. We have to have the anointing and power of Holy Spirit to put into place the verdict that has been rendered.

When we do this as God's anointed vessels and ecclesia, we break the curses that have been legally operating against us. This is our job and position in the process of the Lord to dissolve curses. We take the finished works of the cross and execute them into place so the legal verdict of Calvary has functional power.

Until this is done, we do not get the benefits of what Jesus has accomplished on the cross. The verdict that we are no longer under a curse has been rendered, but until it is forcibly enforced it has no power. This is why we see a discrepancy between what we say we believe and what we actually experience. We see believers dying prematurely who say they believe in healing. We see people bound in poverty who say they believe in prosperity. We see people tormented by demonic forces who say they believe in the peace of God. We see children and family lines being decimated as children walk away from Divine purpose into absolute rebellion and destruction. The issue isn't with what Jesus did on the cross; it is with the execution and enforcement of it into our lives and our world. In other words, curses are still operating even though Jesus annulled them at the cross. The Church has lacked the understanding of the need to enforce His verdict into place.

The truth is that there will always be curses looking for a place to land until Jesus comes back. Revelation, chapter 22, verses 1-3, shows us the heavenly city and its influence in the earth at the coming of the Lord.

> And he showed me a pure river of water of life, clear as crystal, proceeding from the throne of God and of the Lamb. In the middle of its street, and on either side of the river, was the tree of life, which bore twelve fruits, each tree yielding its fruit every month. The leaves of the tree were for the healing of the nations. And there shall be no more curse, but the throne of God and of the Lamb shall be in it, and His servants shall serve Him. (Revelation 22:1-3)

Notice that in this city coming to earth at the coming of the Lord, there is a declaration of "no more curse." In other words, at this point, curses will have no more right to land because of a full execution and enforcement of what Jesus did

Our prayer:

"Now to him who is able to do far more abundantly than all that we ask or think, according to the power at work within us, to him be glory in the church and in Christ Jesus throughout all generations, forever and ever. Amen."
– Ephesians 3:20-21

Transition: Lord, we believe that You can do far more abundantly than we could ever ask or imagine.

Your prayer:

on the cross. The greatness of His sacrifice will have fully been set in place. The full demonstration of all that Jesus legally accomplished on the cross will not be manifest until His coming.

Until that time, we must individually take the sacrifice of the cross and annul the right of curses to operate against our families and us as individuals. Not until the coming of the Lord, will there be "no more curse." This is so important, or else we will keep stating we believe things, we do not experience.

In the springtime in Texas we have what we call "chimney sweeps" that dart about in the air. These are birds that never seem to land anywhere. They fly around constantly. They dive-bomb chimneys on houses, hence the name given to them. Every time I read or think about curses being likened to Sparrows and Swallows, I think about these creatures.

One year, these built a nest right at the front door of our house. The nest was under the awning and out of the weather. These Swallows laid their eggs in this nest. We could go to the front door and look through the window and watch the process of these eggs, as they moved toward the day of their hatching. Pretty soon the baby birds broke through the eggs and came out into the nest. The mother bird cared for them and fed them. It was a marvelous thing to watch UNTIL … they began to poop on everything at our front door.

Now these pretty little birds became menaces that you had to dodge every time you walked out the door. You had to worry about bird poop falling on you or stepping in it on the porch and sidewalk. The wonderful lesson in nature was now replaced with the mess they were creating at the front door of our home. It was bad enough for our family to have to contend with the excrement of these little nuisances, but when visitors and guests came, it was down right embarrassing.

We would have to maneuver people to one side of the porch so they wouldn't become the unwitting target of these little monsters as they relieved themselves. The plan was to tear down the nest as soon as these vultures were old enough to fly away. I was tired and weary of their desecrating my home with what seemed to be a perpetual stream of bird droppings.

The day finally came when they all flew away. I immediately got a broom and went to the front door to quickly tear down this nest. It was made of straw, sticks, grass and some dried mud. It looked very weak and fragile. As I took the sweeping end of the broom and began to prod at the nest, I suddenly realized that the bristles of the broom were not going to take the nest down. It was much stronger and sturdier than it looked. I then took the handle of the broom and begin to poke at the nest. To my amazement it was no match for the strength of this nest.

I went to my garage and found a hoe. I took the hoe and began to poke, then strike and then bang away at this nest that now seemed more like a fort or stronghold. I wondered if the poop had reinforced it. Finally, with much effort, I was able to piece by piece break the nest apart and tear it down. It was difficult, but at least it was now gone and good riddance to these poop-happy birds.

The next spring, these same Swallows came and began to build a nest again. This time when I saw the nest being erected, I tore it down. They would come again and start to piece together the nest. I would go and get my gardening implement and tear it down. It took several times of my destroying what they were trying to build, but they finally stopped and moved somewhere else. I was determined not to have the poop-fest again because these birds were no longer welcomed at my house.

This is exactly what we must do with curses that have landed or want to land in our lives and families. We must not entertain them, no matter how innocent or harmless they may seem. They will become that which will poop on everything if we let them build their nest. They will bring defilement, uncleanness, dismay, discouragement and frustration, if we let them have a place of landing in our lives.

The good news is that if they have landed in our lives there are ways to take away the legal right that has allowed it. We can tear down the nest no matter how strong it may be and remove their defiling effect. We can also prevent them through diligence from building it again. We have been given the authority in the Courts Of Heaven to undo and dissolve everything the devil would use to devour our success and futures. This includes our children and heritage. It also includes our finances, marriages, health and every other important thing.

The remainder of this book is about principles and secrets to getting our generations and us free from curses that want to devour and defile us. Just imagine a life—free from curses—that have sabotaged your future. Now get ready to dream again and step into it. Once curses are removed, nothing shall be impossible.

CHAPTER 2

THE PURPOSE OF CURSES

One of the chief instruments of the devil against us is a curse. If he can find a legal right to land curses against us, then he can sabotage our future and our success. There is a story in the Scriptures about a king named Balak who became very afraid of the nation of Israel, as they passed through his land on their way to their Promise Land. Out of his fear he sends to hire a "prophet" named Balaam to come and curse this nation so he can defeat them. Numbers, chapter 22, verses 5-6, shows us the motive driving his desire for Israel to be cursed.

> Then he sent messengers to Balaam the son of Beor at Pethor, which is near the River in the land of the sons of his people, to call him, saying: "Look, a people has come from Egypt. See, they cover the face of the earth, and are settling next to me! Therefore please come at once, curse this people for me, for they are too mighty for me. Perhaps I shall be able to defeat them and drive them out of the land, for I know that he whom you bless is blessed, and he whom you curse is cursed." (Numbers 22:5-6)

King Balak's reasoning for cursing Israel was so they could be weakened, and he could then defeat them. Without a curse working against them he saw them as too strong to handle. But he felt that if Balaam could put a curse on them, they would be weakened, and he could then defeat them and drive them from his land.

This is the reason the devil desires to have a curse working against us. It weakens us from our place of strength. We are told that in Jesus we are strong. In 1 John, chapter 4, verse 4, it tells us of our strength.

> You are of God, little children, and have overcome them, because He who is in you is greater than he who is in the world. (1 John 4:4)

The One Who lives in us through the person of the Holy Spirit makes us overcomers. No matter what is thrown at us, we beat it and defeat it and always win and triumph. That is unless a curse is working against us to weaken us. Curses working against believers are what allow the ones who are built to overcome to be defeated and lose.

This is why people are sick with chronic disease. This can be why people are prayed for, but still die prematurely. This can be why families come to financial ruin. This can be why tragedy runs through families from generation to generation. This can be why divorce happens in family lines over and over again. This is why devastating sin patterns repeat themselves for generations to come, and actually, grow worse and worse. All of this and so much more can be the result of curses working to weaken us so we can be defeated. Deuteronomy, chapter 28, verse 45, tells us the predictive pattern of any curse that is not dealt with.

> Moreover all these curses shall come upon you and pursue and overtake you, until you are destroyed, because you did not obey the voice of the LORD your God, to keep His commandments and His statutes which He commanded you. (Deuteronomy 28:45)

This Scripture mentions four stages of a curse:
- It comes upon us
- Pursues us
- Overtakes us
- Destroys us

This means that curses are aggressive in their activities against us. They are not content until they have completely destroyed life and destinies. Curses do not stop, until we stop them. We cannot outlast them or endure them until they end. We must proactively stop them and their operation. We see this in the life of a man named Jeroboam.

One of the main purposes of a curse is to annihilate family lines and their purpose from the earth. In 1 Kings, chapter 13, verse 34, it tells us the curse that landed on Jeroboam and his family as a consequence of his sin.

> And this thing was the sin of the house of Jeroboam, so as to exterminate and destroy it from the face of the earth. (1 Kings 13:34)

God intends to touch the earth through families. The Lord lays his hand upon the family and family lines to carry certain things connected to His Kingdom purpose. If the devil can get a curse operating against a family, he can stop that purpose from being fulfilled. He can stop what God intended to enter the earth through that family from occurring.

This is what happened to the family of Jeroboam. Jeroboam was chosen by God to be King of Israel. But his fear of people forsaking him and reverting back to the former dynasty of Solomon and his sons drove him to set up a religious system that was not ordained of the Lord. He set up another place of worship, with a separate priesthood and different offerings. This was to keep the people from returning to Jerusalem and the feast ordained by God to worship. This was severely offensive to the Lord. The result was a curse coming on his family and him. This sin opened the door and gave legal right for a curse to land that exterminated his family from the earth.

This is the ultimate reason for curses. The devil likes nothing better than to actually remove a family line from the earth and stop its Kingdom purpose. But if he cannot do that completely, he will use curses to stop the reason for the family in the earth. In other words, if he cannot exterminate them literally, he will steal away and exterminate the purpose why God wanted them in the earth. Satan uses curses to do this. Through curses the effect God intended through a family can be completely destroyed. This is a great motivation for Satan to find legal right to land curses against us.

We speak much about generational curses and rightly so. But the reason for generational curses is because Satan is seeking to stop the generational blessing from flowing. God chooses family lines to move through. He chooses houses to exercise Kingdom rule. Every family line born into the earth has a Kingdom purpose attached to it. Paul told Timothy that the Kingdom purpose they were to live out was established before time began. 2 Timothy, chapter 1, verse 9, reveals this awesome truth.

> Who has saved us and called us with a holy calling, not according to our works, but according to His own purpose and grace which was given to us in Christ Jesus before time began ... (2 Timothy 1:9)

Notice that purpose and grace was given to us before time began. Purpose is our reason for existence and grace is the empowerment to accomplish it. Before anything existed, the earth, sun, moon, stars, time and even the planets, God ordained our existence and purpose. He also appointed grace connected to that purpose so we would be empowered to fulfill it. This is why anything we are called to do we have the ability. When we discover our purpose we know it because of the grace or supernatural empowerment that is attached to it.

Paul is instructing Timothy concerning this timeless truth. Timothy had received, as a part of his family inheritance, a tremendous faith. His grandmother, Lois, and mother, Eunice, carried a faith that had been passed down to him.

> When I call to remembrance the genuine faith that is in you, which dwelt first in your grandmother Lois and your mother Eunice, and I am persuaded is in you also. (2 Timothy 1:5)

Timothy had a faith that was a part of his family line. Timothy was meant by God to demonstrate and operate in a faith that manifested the Kingdom of God. Yet there was also a fear and timidity in Timothy that warred against the demonstration of this faith. In 2 Timothy, chapter 1, verses 6-7, we see Paul seeking to break the spirit of fear off of Timothy that wants to stop the manifestation of this inherited faith.

Therefore I remind you to stir up the gift of God which is in you through the laying on of my hands. For God has not given us a spirit of fear, but of power and of love and of a sound mind. (2 Timothy 1:6-7)

This spirit of fear or timidity is a curse, seeking to stop this supernatural realm of faith from operating out of the family line. There had to be a recognizing that this was not just a personality issue, but a curse working against Timothy to stop the release of the family blessing into the earth. The words "stir up" means a fire that is kindled and/or a live thing, a beast. Paul was telling Timothy to become aggressive against this curse that was seeking to stop the realm of faith from operating through him. He was saying release the power of faith that was on the inside of him as a result of the generational blessing he was carrying. Let the flame of it consume the fear and timidity. Literally, release the beast that was on the inside of Timothy to break this curse that wanted to turn him into something that he wasn't. He needed to destroy that which wanted to make him weak and timid, instead of bold and powerful.

I know something about this spirit of timidity. It runs through my family line. Now I preach and speak the Word of God to many people and even nations. That wasn't always the case. My wife tells the story of when we were dating and how bashful and shy I was. She relates that when we would go to a restaurant on our dates, I wouldn't even speak to the waiter or waitress. I was so timid I would not even order my food and drink. She would have to do it for me! My earthly father was very much like this, as well as some of my siblings. There was a spirit of fear and timidity that sought to warp my personality.

Thank God that Jesus breaks curses and frees us so we can fulfill our destinies. The destiny of God for my life is to preach the Gospel and disciple nations. Yet, the curse of timidity in the family line would have liked to distort and disturb that call. So in addition to generational curses working against us, we also carry generational or family blessings. We need to discover these and deal with every curse that wants to diminish or destroy them and destroy it instead. When we do, we will begin to step into destiny and purpose.

Everything has a Kingdom purpose attached to it. Individuals, families, cities, states and nations all carry Divine purpose. The devil uses curses to stop any and all of these from reaching their destinies. We can see this concerning the city of Jericho in Scripture. Jericho was the first city of conquest as the children of Israel took the Promise Land. After the city was completely destroyed, Joshua leveled a curse over this city. Joshua, chapter 6, verse 26, reveals the curse spoken concerning the rebuilding of Jericho.

Then Joshua charged them at that time, saying, "Cursed be the man before the LORD who rises up and builds this city Jericho; he shall lay its foundation with his firstborn, and with his youngest he shall set up its gates." (Joshua 6:26)

This curse had its effect in 1 Kings, chapter 16, verse 34.

In his days Hiel of Bethel built Jericho. He laid its foundation with Abiram his firstborn, and with his youngest son Segub he set up its gates, according to the word of the LORD, which He had spoken through Joshua the son of Nun. (1 Kings 16:34)

Hiel rebuilt the city of Jericho at the cost of the life of his firstborn and youngest sons because of the curse against Jericho that Joshua had spoken. Five hundred years later this curse resulted in the death of two men. This curse continued to operate for generations to come. Even though Jericho was rebuilt, there was still a curse operating against this city. We see this in 2 Kings, chapter 2, verses 19-22. After Elisha has received the mantle from Elijah, the men of Jericho beseeched him to remove the lingering curse.

Then the men of the city said to Elisha, "Please notice, the situation of this city is pleasant, as my lord sees; but the water is bad, and the ground barren." And he said, "Bring me a new bowl, and put salt in it." So they brought it to him. Then he went out to the source of the water, and cast in the salt there, and said, "Thus says the LORD: 'I have healed this water; from it there shall be no more death or barrenness.'" So the water remains healed to this day, according to the word of Elisha which he spoke. (2 Kings 2:19-22)

Elisha was able to remove the curse that now made an otherwise city pleasant. The word *barren* means to bereave of children. It wasn't that the land would not just produce crops, it was that in the land, children were dying. The curse that had been spoken by Joshua was still granting a legal right to kill people prematurely. We know this is true because this is what Elisha rebuked when he removed the curse. He said, "from it there shall be no more death or barrenness." Again the word *barren* means to bereave of children, to rob of children, to miscarry and lose children. The word *death* means by natural occurrence or violence. There clearly was a wave of ongoing destruction in the city that resulted in loss of life after loss of life. People of the city were asking Elisha to please remove this death curse from this city. It is interesting how Elisha removed this curse.

There were several "steps" to dissolving this curse

from this city. The first thing is the men asked Elijah to "please notice" the state of the city. This word or phrase actually means "a seat." They were asking Elisha to speak and remove the curse over this city from "the seat" he occupied in the spirit realm. When Elisha received the mantle from Elijah, he sat down in a seat in the spirit realm. This is what the Lord was speaking of when He promised we could sit in His throne. Revelation, chapter 3, verse 21, declares this is a reward to the overcomers.

> To him who overcomes I will grant to sit with Me
> on My throne, as I also overcame and sat down
> with My Father on His throne. (Revelation 3:21)

This was not speaking of the afterlife or Heaven. This is speaking of a place we can occupy in the spirit realm now. When we are dealing with curses over cities, regions, states or nations, they must be removed and dissolved by someone in a seat in the spirit realm. I teach that we can function from one of three dimensions. We can function from an anointing, authority or a seat of government, which is a throne. The anointing level is a result of a gift. The authority level is a result of right alignment with God and those who represent God into our lives. The seat of government or throne in the spirit realm is a result of overcoming. When we live an overcoming life, we can be granted a seat in the spirit realm. From this seat we can undo curses from off of people and regions.

I have had several dreams about being in seats. Probably the most significant one was when what I understood to be angelic beings were dispatched to cleanse my spiritual walk. This particular being had an instrument in his hand that he put into my shoes while they were on my feet. With this instrument he cleansed my walk to a new place. Once this was done, suddenly there was a "seat" that was hovering in the atmosphere. I sat down in this seat. It had controls that would cause the seat to move.

I remember touching the controls and realizing how powerful this seat was that I was in. This angelic being, again appeared. He began to teach me how to "move in the seat." We must not only take a seat given to us, we must also know how to "move in it." As I was sitting in this seat, this angelic being presented me with a check. On the check were demands and points of obedience I had to walk in to move in this seat. I knew that because these places of obedience were given to me in a check form, that I was being given the grace to walk in these places of obedience.

From this time on, I have walked in these points of obedience, which has qualified me as an overcomer. This provides me with the privilege to sit in this seat and see breakthroughs come from it. This seat has given me the right to proclaim curses dissolved and blessing established. This is what the people of Jericho understood concerning Elisha. May we find our seat in the spirit realm and function from it to see curses dissolved.

The next thing Elisha did to remove this curse was he asked for a new bowl. The word *bowl* literally means a vial. It comes from a word that means to break out or press forward. To deal with curses we must have a heart to move forward. Curses keep us stuck and bogged down. We must have an aggressive spirit that wants to break free. Curses can create a lethargic attitude that keeps us bound. We must be stirred in our spirits to become free from curses. I am reminded of what Isaac prophesied over Esau after Jacob had stolen the blessing away. Genesis, chapter 27, verse 40 says Esau was going to have to become weary of what was limiting him before he could become free.

> And it shall come to pass, when you become restless, That you shall break his yoke from your neck. (Genesis 27:40)

Before Esau could get free from the restraints that were holding him, he had to become restless. He had to become weary in his spirit of the limits that were on him. The Spirit of the Lord within us must stir us to desire something more than what a curse has allowed us to become. It takes an aggressive spirit and attitude to break out and move forward and see curses dissolved.

Elisha also called for salt to be put into this new bowl. Salt was a sign of judgment and covenant. Judges, chapter 9, verse 45, shows that sowing salt on a land was a judgment.

> So Abimelech fought against the city all that day;
> he took the city and killed the people who were in
> it; and he demolished the city and sowed it with
> salt. (Judges 9:45)

The sowing of salt was to make the ground barren and unable to produce for generations to come. Salt was also a sign of our covenant with God. Leviticus, chapter 2, verse 13, commands that every offering was to have salt added to it.

> And every offering of your grain offering you
> shall season with salt; you shall not allow the salt
> of the covenant of your God to be lacking from
> your grain offering. With all your offerings you
> shall offer salt. (Leviticus 2:13)

Salt spoke of the covenant with God that was had. When Elisha required salt, he was judging what had been afflicting this city for generations. He was also reminding and enacting the covenant with God through the use of salt. He was asking and decreeing on the bases of covenant for the curse that was bringing death to the children to be removed that Joshua had placed on the city. From our covenantal position that Jesus bought for us at the cross, we can judge everything that is stopping blessings from flowing. We can dissolve curses that are allowing death in any form to operate. This is our place as New Testament believers. Romans, chapter 12, verse 14, declares that we are to bless and curse not.

> Bless those who persecute you; bless and do not
> curse. (Romans 12:14)

Sometimes it is easy to get on the negative side of things. We must take the authority we have been given and use it for good. We are called by God to undo curses that are plaguing people, even nations. Once we do this, we set them free to move into the destinies planned for them by God.

Elisha then went to the source of the water supply of the city. When we are dealing with a curse we must find the source that is allowing it to operate. By going to the source of the water supply Elisha was symbolically declaring he was cutting the root of the curse. What had operated in the spirit realm for generations was now being undone.

The last thing Elisha did to dissolve this curse off the city of Jericho was he decreed with great authority. He declared that he had healed the waters and death and barrenness could no longer operate. When we are in our seat in the spirit realm, from this place decrees can be made that alter spiritual realities. The result of Elisha's decree was the waters being healed permanently. It wasn't a temporary fix. What had been operating for generations was completely eradicated and removed. This was so much so that Jericho became known as a place of great blessings. Once the waters were healed, death stopped and fruitfulness came. The city became known as the city of palm trees. In 2 Chronicles, chapter 28, verse 15, it speaks of this city.

> Then the men who were designated by name rose up and took the captives, and from the spoil they clothed all who were naked among them, dressed them and gave them sandals, gave them food and drink, and anointed them; and they let all the feeble ones ride on donkeys. So they brought them to their brethren at Jericho, the city of palm trees. Then they returned to Samaria.

Jericho became known as a place of life, refreshing, recovery and fruitfulness. This all happened because Elisha removed the curse that had operated against it for generations. This is the same authority and power that the Lord has released today from the cross of Jesus. May we move in this dimension to see curses removed and blessings established.

In the next chapters, we will discover the source of many curses and how to take away their legal right to operate. Without finding the source of a curse we are only dealing with the symptoms. God will grant us wisdom to discern why a curse is operating and how to dissolve it.

CHAPTER 3

THE SOURCES OF CURSES

As I mentioned in the beginning of this book, curses are legal in their nature. This is why Proverbs, chapter 26, verse 2, says they have to have a cause to land.

> Like a flitting sparrow, like a flying swallow, So a curse without cause shall not alight. (Proverbs 26:2)

The cause is something that in the spirit realm has given the devil the legal right to afflict with a curse. This curse can result in a myriad of issues against our lives, if we do not know how to undo it. Every person and every family has curses that potentially operate against them. None are exempt from this. The reason for this is because of where curses come from and what gives them the legal right to work against us.

Curses are in general the result of sin, transgression and iniquity. These are biblical words that must be understood. When the Bible speaks of sin, it uses these three different words to describe this activity. Psalm, chapter 32, verses 1-2, use these three words.

> Blessed is he whose transgression is forgiven,
> Whose sin is covered. Blessed is the man to
> whom the LORD does not impute iniquity, And
> in whose spirit there is no deceit. (Psalm 32:1-2)

David also spoke of these three words in Psalm, chapter 51, verses 1-2.

> Have mercy upon me, O God, According to Your
> lovingkindness; According to the multitude of
> Your tender mercies, Blot out my transgressions.
> Wash me thoroughly from my iniquity, And
> cleanse me from my sin. (Psalm 51:1-2)

If we are going to gain understanding of the legal places that curses can use to land, we must understand the inherent meaning of the words sin, transgression and iniquity.

Sin is the Hebrew word *chata'ah*. It comes from the root word *chata* and means *to miss*. Romans, chapter 3, verse 23, tells us that sin is falling short of the glory of God.

> For all have sinned and fall short of the glory of
> God ... (Romans 3:23)

This word *sinned* is the Greek word *hamartano*, and it means to miss the mark and not share in the prize. So sin will cause us not to get the inheritance that was intended for us by God. Some have described sin as not just an activity, but a purposing and intention of the mind. In other words, when I decide to sin, but haven't had the opportunity yet, I have already offended God. Romans, chapter 8, verse 7, declares that our minds, when in an unredeemed state, are enemies and at enmity with God.

> Because the carnal mind is enmity against God;
> for it is not subject to the law of God, nor indeed
> can be. (Romans 8:7)

So in our minds we can be enemies of God and be planning unrighteous things. This can be sin, before any activity is ever practiced. We must repent of even the intentions of our mind before the Lord.

Jesus spoke of this in Matthew, chapter 5, verses 27-28, when He was dealing with the lust issue.

> "You have heard that it was said to those of old,
> 'You shall not commit adultery.' But I say to you
> that whoever looks at a woman to lust for her
> has already committed adultery with her in his
> heart." (Matthew 5:27-28)

There was no activity of adultery here, just the fantasy

of it in the mind. To involve oneself with these ideas in the mind is to "sin" against the Lord. We must deal with the secrets of the heart and the issues of the mind to be clean before the Lord. Lest we excuse ourselves from this, we should realize that Job found himself in great trouble because Satan landed a curse against him based on the accusations of impure motives. Job, chapter 1, verses 8-12, shows this discourse between God and Satan that gave Satan the legal right to land trouble and curses against Job.

> Then the LORD said to Satan, "Have you considered My servant Job, that there is none like him on the earth, a blameless and upright man, one who fears God and shuns evil?" So Satan answered the LORD and said, "Does Job fear God for nothing? Have You not made a hedge around him, around his household, and around all that he has on every side? You have blessed the work of his hands, and his possessions have increased in the land. But now, stretch out Your hand and touch all that he has, and he will surely curse You to Your face!" And the LORD said to Satan, "Behold, all that he has is in your power; only do not lay a hand on his person." So Satan went out from the presence of the LORD. (Job 1:8-12)

When Satan made an accusation against Job, concerning the motives that Job was serving God with a legal right was found to land the curses. Job had DONE nothing wrong. The accusation was against anything in the mind and motives. We must repent before the Lord of even the hidden things of our mind. These can be used to bring curses against us.

The second word used is transgression. This is the Hebrew word *pasha,* and it means a revolt or rebellion, to break away from just authority. It also carries the idea of expansion. It is activity that leads to more and more wickedness and evil. It also means to stride or spread the legs in walking. It is crossing over the lines and boundaries set by the Lord. Someone once said that, "Christians have chalk dust on their toes from walking to close to lines they aren't suppose to be crossing."

This is rebellion that would even allow this activity. If the sin of the mind can be legal places for curses, how much more the actual activity of sin. We must repent for every activity of rebellion. In fact, when we give in to the activities of the flesh, the thing driving it almost always is rebellion. We are saying to God, "I don't care what You want, I'm going to do what I want." This is rebellion and revolt. When I repent of sins of lust, anger, attitudes and other things against the Lord, almost always at its root is rebellion. I not only have to repent of the activity, but the root cause of rebellion in my heart that allowed it. Transgression not repented of can give curses legal rights to land.

The third word used here is iniquity. This is the Hebrew word *avon* and it means perversity, to be crooked. It speaks not just of an activity, but of a nature. It means a propensity toward a certain sin. Iniquity is the result of sin in the bloodline. God said that He would visit the iniquity upon the third and fourth generation.

> "You shall not bow down to them nor serve them. For I, the LORD your God, am a jealous God, visiting the iniquity of the fathers upon the children to the third and fourth generations of those who hate Me, but showing mercy to thousands, to those who love Me and keep My commandments." (Exodus 20:5-6)

If someone in our bloodline gave themselves over to a sin, this can create an iniquity that can work against us. This is why people find themselves tempted with things very strongly. It is the result of activities of our ancestors. Their activity allows the devil to work against us legally.

Many people that do not understand this phenomenon want to declare that when Jesus died on the cross, these issues of iniquity were dealt with. I want to remind us that what Jesus did on the cross does render a verdict against iniquity and its power, but we must execute it into place. The devil is a legalist and will continue to use iniquity as a legal reason to land curses until we forcibly stop him. We can see this in Ezekiel, chapter 18, verses 1-4.

> The word of the LORD came to me again, saying, "What do you mean when you use this proverb concerning the land of Israel, saying: 'The fathers have eaten sour grapes, And the children's teeth are set on edge?'
>
> "As I live," says the Lord GOD, "you shall no longer use this proverb in Israel.
>
> "Behold, all souls are Mine; The soul of the father As well as the soul of the son is Mine; The soul who sins shall die." (Ezekiel 18:1-4)

This Scripture appears to state that the law-of-iniquity will no longer work. It seems to be saying that the fathers' sins will have no more affect on us. What is not understood sometimes is this is God's desire and intent expressed. Most prophecy is the intent of God declared. It is our responsibility to take the intent and bring it into reality. We see this in Ezekiel, chapter 36, verse 36-37.

> "Then the nations which are left all around you shall know that I, the LORD, have rebuilt the ruined places and planted what was desolate. I, the LORD, have spoken it, and I will do it.

'Thus says the Lord GOD: "I will also let the house of Israel inquire of Me to do this for them: I will increase their men like a flock." (Ezekiel 36:36-37)

God is making great promises to Israel about its future. He declares that He will allow them as a people to pray His intent into reality. This is almost always the case. God makes promises, and then says it is our responsibility to bring them into reality through our spiritual activity.

This is also what is happening in Ezekiel, chapter 18. He is promising and declaring that the sins of the forefathers will not destroy their future. This is the heart of God. But we must put this intent into legal place or curses can land against us from the iniquity of our bloodline. We see this as we finish Ezekiel, chapter 18, verse 30.

"Therefore I will judge you, O house of Israel, every one according to his ways," says the Lord GOD. "Repent, and turn from all your transgressions, so that iniquity will not be your ruin." (Ezekiel 18:30)

At the beginning of Ezekiel, chapter 18, God is saying that there will be no sins of the fathers working against them. Yet, at the end of Ezekiel 18, God is saying they must repent and turn, or iniquity, which is the sin of the bloodline, will be their ruin. Clearly God is declaring that His passion is that the sins of the fathers will not destroy them. They must repent or those sins will be their ruin.

In others words, their destiny and future will be forfeited because of the effects of iniquity working against them. We must put into effect the prophetic intent of God so we get the benefits of it working in our behalf.

Iniquity not dealt with will ruin our future. Iniquity allows curses the legal right to land. Iniquity has at least four devastating effects against us. The first effect is iniquity grants the devil the legal right to tempt us in a given area. When someone in our family history gives themselves over to a certain sin, this grants the devil the legal right to tempt us with that same thing. The source of the temptation is the failure of those from our family history.

To describe this let me use a personal example. When I was three or four years old, we would receive the Sears and Roebuck catalogue in the mail. This was in the 1960's. As a small child I loved it when this catalogue came to our house. I would take the catalogue and look at all the toys and dream of what I might get at Christmas time. But I did something else with this catalogue. I would take it and go behind a chair or into a corner and find the women's section. I would then look at the women in their underwear. I liked to look at the women in their underwear at three and four years old.

Where does a child this age get a desire to see women in their underwear? Nothing like this went on in our house. I had never been exposed to sexual issues or deviate practices. Where did this temptation come from that I faced at such an early age? It came from the sin of my bloodline that allowed iniquity to work against me. Someone in my bloodline had given themselves to sexual uncleanness, and it opened the door for the devil to tempt me in this area.

Every family has iniquity working in its family history. Iniquity is the result of sins operated in from the ancestry. This can make these temptations very powerful. This is why we see the same sins committed from generation to generation where they were "unlearned." We see this is the life of Abraham and his son, Isaac. In Genesis, chapter 12, verses 10-13.

> Now there was a famine in the land, and Abram went down to Egypt to dwell there, for the famine was severe in the land. And it came to pass, when he was close to entering Egypt, that he said to Sarai his wife, "Indeed I know that you are a woman of beautiful countenance." Therefore it will happen, when the Egyptians see you, that they will say, 'This is his wife;' and they will kill me, but they will let you live. "Please say you are my sister, that it may be well with me for your sake, and that I may live because of you" (Genesis 12:10-13)

Abraham concocted a plan to have Sarai say she was his sister for fear of him being killed, so they could take her to be his wife. It is recorded that Abraham actually did this twice. We find it again in Genesis, chapter 20, verse 2.

> "Now Abraham said of Sarah his wife, 'She is my sister.' And Abimelech king of Gerar sent and took Sarah." (Genesis 20:2)

Abraham's fear caused him to place Sarah in a very perilous position, as they entered different nations and kingdoms. This was a sin that was born out of fear. It was full of selfishness and disgrace. God always protected Sarah in these situations, but that didn't alleviate the sin of Abraham.

Many decades later, after Isaac was born, he committed the same sins with his wife, Rebekah. Genesis, chapter 26, verses 6-7, shows Isaac doing the same thing.

> So Isaac dwelt in Gerar. And the men of the place asked about his wife. And he said, "She is my sister;" for he was afraid to say, "She is my wife," because he thought, "lest the men of the place kill me for Rebekah, because she is beautiful to behold." (Genesis 26:6-7)

Isaac was not alive when Abraham placed Sarah in the

dangerous position by his lies; yet, he repeats the same error. Without being instructed, influenced or persuaded in the natural in any way, Isaac falls prey to the same sins as his father. He repeats his father's sins. This is what iniquity does. It causes generations to repeat the sins of the fathers over and over. It gives the devil the legal right to tempt successive generations with the same sins the fathers fell pray to.

If we can understand this, we can take the blood of Jesus and deal with the powerful force of iniquity that wants to work against us. David spoke of this when he said he kept himself from iniquity. Psalm, chapter 18, verse 23, declares that David had a confidence that God would answer his prayers because he had not yielded to the power of iniquity working against him.

"I was also blameless before Him, And I kept myself from my iniquity." (Psalm 18:23)

The temptation of the devil had a pull on David as a result of the iniquity of his family lineage. David in these moments withstood the power of these temptations. When the iniquity is broken, it doesn't mean we will not be tempted. It simply means we have the ability to say, "No!" to the temptation. Even Jesus was tempted, yet without sin. Jesus had no sin nature or iniquity working in Him from His bloodline. His bloodline is perfect because it is from the Father. Yet, Jesus was tempted.

The sign of a sin nature or iniquity is not temptation.

The sign of a sin nature working in us is the inability to say, "No" to sin. When we take the blood of Jesus and deal with not just sin and transgression, but iniquity as well, we can dissolve the power of temptation against us.

A second thing iniquity does is it shapes our identity. My definition for identity is, "the inner most thoughts I think about myself." A proper identity will believe the things God believes about us. The problem is that iniquity shapes our beliefs about ourselves. We see this in the life of Isaiah. In Isaiah, chapter 6, verses 1-8, we see God graciously dealing with the iniquity that is fashioning the way Isaiah thinks about himself.

> In the year that King Uzziah died, I saw the Lord sitting on a throne, high and lifted up, and the train of His robe filled the temple. Above it stood seraphim; each one had six wings: with two he covered his face, with two he covered his feet, and with two he flew. And one cried to another and said: "Holy, holy, holy is the LORD of hosts; The whole earth is full of His glory!" And the posts of the door were shaken by the voice of him who cried out, and the house was filled with smoke. So I said: "Woe is me, for I am undone! Because I am a man of unclean lips, And I dwell in the midst of a people of unclean lips; For my eyes have seen the King, The LORD of hosts."

Then one of the seraphim flew to me, having in his hand a live coal which he had taken with the tongs from the altar. And he touched my mouth with it, and said: "Behold, this has touched your lips; Your iniquity is taken away, And your sin purged." Also I heard the voice of the Lord, saying: "Whom shall I send, And who will go for Us?" Then I said, "Here am I! Send me." (Isaiah 6:1-8)

Isaiah saw himself as sinful, undone and unworthy. Notice that it was iniquity that the angelic being cleansed him from with the coal. The iniquity that was operating against him caused him to see himself as unworthy. Once the iniquity is cleansed two main things happened. He was able to hear the Lord and feel His passion. Iniquity and its effects block us from perceiving spiritually what is happening. We do not see the way God really feels about us. This leads to the second thing that happens.

When the cleansing occurred it also dealt with the unworthiness Isaiah was feeling. Isaiah is declaring himself to be unclean, undone and unworthy. He is feeling as if he can't be used of God. Once the iniquity is purged, he has a new sense of identity that propels him to volunteer to go for the Lord. He no longer sees himself as an unworthy vessel, but as one qualified to go for the Lord. This is a picture of what happens once our identity is free from the shaping of iniquity. We see ourselves the way God sees us and are free to be his servants.

The bottom line is that iniquity operating against us is used by the devil to lie to us about who we really are. People believe these lies all the time. They become sexually unclean. They become alcoholics and substance abusers. They become controlled by poverty. They end up living a life far below the intent of God for them and their families. Once the power of iniquity is broken, they are transformed in their thinking. They are free to be who God made them to be.

The third thing that iniquity does is it warps the original intent of God and what is written in the books of Heaven about us. Psalm, chapter 139, verse 16, states that all of us have destinies written in books in Heaven.

> Your eyes saw my substance, being yet unformed.
> And in Your book they all were written, The days
> fashioned for me, When as yet there were none of
> them. (Psalm 139:16)

The length of our days and what we are to accomplish in them were written in books or scrolls in Heaven. Our purpose is to discover what is in our book and flesh it out in the earth. Before we existed in the earth, we were a scroll in Heaven. If our destinies are written in books or scrolls in Heaven, then the day we were born, we landed as a scroll from Heaven in a fleshly body. We are to spend the rest of our days discovering what is written in the scroll and fleshing it.

The problem is what originated from Heaven in the scroll landed in a body connected to a bloodline. The devil uses the iniquity of the bloodline to seek to warp and detour us from what has been written in the books of Heaven about us. He uses iniquity to take us off course from our God-intended purpose.

To make the point concerning this, I wonder how many homeless people living under bridges were destined to bring breakthrough to the human race. Perhaps one who was intended to cure cancer, instead found themselves ravished through alcoholism, mental illness, drug addictions or other personal trauma. The devil used the iniquity of their bloodline to stop the destiny intended for them in their scrolls. Not only did they suffer, but mankind was denied the breakthroughs and the purposes of God were frustrated. This is one of the results of iniquity at work.

The fourth thing iniquity does is grant the devil the legal right to build cases that result in curses operating against us. Curses are the result of legal cases against us in the spirit realm.

Just to illustrate the devil's use of curses to sabotage destiny and futures let me share a personal experience of my wife and me.

I was away on a ministry trip and had a very powerful dream. In my dream my wife, Mary, and I were in a certain setting. As we stood, Mary's aunt, whose name was Mildred, appeared standing behind Mary. Mildred has been dead and with the Lord for many years. In the dream I knew she was there as a part of the "Great Cloud of Witnesses." (Hebrews 12:1)

Mary began to speak and say, "I'm getting stronger and stronger." As she is speaking, Mildred is shaking her head in disagreement. I knew she was saying Mary was in fact getting "weaker and weaker" and would die prematurely. My sense in the dream was that there was a legal scheme against Mary and the women of her bloodline to cause her to die prematurely.

When I awoke from the dream, I decided not to tell Mary, but to just pray about it. I didn't want to upset her with this kind of dream. About two weeks later my daughter, Sarah, called me. She said she had a dream about Mary, her Mom. In her dream Mary had a heart attack and was in the hospital getting "weaker and weaker" and was going to die. When she told me the dream I knew God was urging me to bring this curse to the Courts of Heaven so it didn't bring premature death.

I then told Mary the dreams. I reminded her that her Mom died at 58 years old. She then told me her grandmother died in her 40's, which I did not know. There was clearly a pattern of a curse working against the women of her bloodline. I contacted someone who has a seer gift that I know and asked if she could help Mary and me cleanse anything in her bloodline that would allow this to happen. She agreed.

As we began the session of presenting Mary and her bloodline before the Lord, Mary laid her life down before the

Lord all the way back to Adam and Eve. This is where all our bloodlines extend to. Some say they can only go back three to four generations. The fourth generation of your bloodline is connected to another four and another four all the way back to Adam and Eve. It is safe to deal with anything legal all the way back to this place.

As Mary prayed the seer began to see issues concerning Masonry in her bloodline. Mary confirmed that her grandfather had been a Mason. The seer also saw women who were "breeders" for Masons. My understanding is these were women who were used for sexual pleasure and to propagate children for the Masons. It was a very perverse thing. Some of the women in Mary's bloodline had been these "breeders." The result was the devil had a case against the women of the bloodline to cause them to die prematurely.

Mary prayed and repented for herself, her bloodline and the connection to Free Masonry, especially this whole "breeder" thing. When we were finished there was a deep sense that a legal issue to cause Mary to die prematurely was now removed. The work of the Cross had again prevailed against the legal right of the devil to curse! The case against Mary and her bloodline that had come from iniquity was now removed. Thank God for His mercies and grace that allows us to triumph over any and every case of the enemy.

You may have some questions about how to detect if there is actual a curse on your life. In the next chapter we will talk about some of the signs of curses at work.

CHAPTER 4

SIGNS AND TRAITS OF CURSES

Sometimes we miss the fact that curses are operating against us. We think they are just the normal parts of our life. In fact, I believe we get so use to living with curses working against us that we accept them. This is what it appears David did in 2 Samuel, chapter 21, verse 1.

> Now there was a famine in the days of David for three years, year after year; and David inquired of the LORD. And the LORD answered, "It is because of Saul and his bloodthirsty house, because he killed the Gibeonites." (2 Samuel 21:1)

There had been a famine working against Israel for three years. It seems, perhaps, for the first year David didn't think anything about it. After all, you can have a year of diminished rain. Then it occurs the second year. Now the effects of the drought are getting much more serious. Then it happens the third year, and David inquires of the Lord. It was the third year before David began to think something spiritual was the root of the problem. He then asked the Lord and God told him it was because of Saul breaking covenant with the Gibeonites.

David then deals with the broken covenant the devil is legally using to bring this famine. God is now able to heed the prayers for the land. The main point is that it took three years for David to recognize he wasn't dealing with something natural, but rather with a curse that was working against them.

How often is this our case? We see difficulties come. We think they are just natural occurrences. The result is that things get worse and worse because we have not recognized the real issue at work. A curse is operating against us, and we think it is just a natural problem, rather than spiritual dilemma.

One of the first steps in dealing with curses is recognizing their existence. In Deuteronomy, chapter 28, there is a list of things that occur when curses are present. I realize that Jesus delivered us from the curse of the law. According to Galatians, chapter 3, verse 13, Jesus became a curse for us and set us free.

> Christ has redeemed us from the curse of the law, having become a curse for us (for it is written, "Cursed is everyone who hangs on a tree,") (Galatians 3:13)

Jesus dealt with the legal issue that allows curses to operate. Yet, remember that in Revelation, chapter 22, verse 3, we are told only in the millennial reign of Jesus will there be no more curse.

And there shall be no more curse, but the throne of God and of the Lamb shall be in it, and His servants shall serve Him. (Revelation 22:3)

Only at the millennial reign of Jesus will there be a wholesale removal of curses. Up until this time, we must take the legal, finished work of Jesus on the cross and execute that verdict into place personally. When we do this by faith, through our repentance, decrees and spiritual activities, we become free from curses and their effects. We possess the abundant life that Jesus said we were to live. Success and prosperity in every dimension of our lives begins to manifest.

To deal with curses we must learn to recognize their existence. Let's take a look at Deuteronomy, chapter 28, and see some of the characteristics of curses at work. There are twelve traits that help us determine a curse operating against us.

1. The first thing a curse does is it creates a negative mindset and mentality. Instead of expecting good to come and having a positive outlook on life, we anticipate evil. Deuteronomy, chapter 28, verse 66, shows a pessimistic view of our future as a result of a curse.

    Your life shall hang in doubt before you; you shall fear day and night, and have no assurance of life. (Deuteronomy 28:66)

A curse causes us to live life without vision for the future. We can actually expect evil to come, rather than good. This is because a curse has fashioned the way we see life. This mindset can beset a whole family line. There is a negativity that saps any real faith for the future. As a result of this nothing exceptional is attempted. The pessimistic view of life sentences us to live well below what God intended. To see this reversed, we must deal with the curse that is allowing this mindset to operate in the family. Once the curse is broken and dissolved, vision will ignite, faith will arise and devilish limitations will come off.

2. A second trait connected to a curse is you can't seem to escape it. No matter where you are you can't get away from it. Bad things seem to chase you down. Deuteronomy, chapter 28, verse 19, says whether you are going out or coming in there is a curse there.

> Cursed shall you be when you come in,
> and cursed shall you be when you go out.
> (Deuteronomy 28:19)

It seems nothing works for you. No matter how promising things seem to be, they always fall apart. There seems to be something that sabotages every hopeful thing concerning your future. There is an invisible conspiracy against you that will not allow you to succeed. This is a sign of a curse. Once it is removed, the same efforts will bring success that have failed in the past. It isn't an issue of effort. It is a curse in the unseen realm, that when removed, can no longer stop your destiny from happening.

3. A third sign of a curse is no vision for life. Deuteronomy, chapter 28, verse 29, shows that a curse causes there to be no vision or purpose for life. You literally live life as one who is blind and gropes in the darkness.

> And you shall grope at noonday, as a blind man gropes in darkness; you shall not prosper in your ways; you shall be only oppressed and plundered continually, and no one shall save you. (Deuteronomy 28:29)

People who are beset by curses have a problem living life with vision. They have no sense of destiny. They live with aimlessness. That is, they have no real target they are shooting for.

Throughout my years in ministry, I have had staff members who wanted me to tell them what their destiny and purpose was. They had no real sense of purpose for their life. I now know this is a sign of a curse being over lives. The curse that was on their lives actually created a blindness that would not allow them to discern destiny. The word *blind* from the root in the Hebrew means to have a film over the eyes. This is what a curse is. It is like a film over the eyes, stopping vision from developing.

The answer is to dissolve the curse. Once this is done a progressive revelation of destiny and purpose will manifest. They will begin to see with new eyes the reason they exist. Destiny and vision will explode from their spirit.

4. The fourth trait of a curse is a breakdown of marriages and homes. Deuteronomy, chapter 28, verse 30 shows that a curse causes broken hearts and destruction of marriages.

> You shall betroth a wife, but another man shall lie with her; you shall build a house, but you shall not dwell in it ... (Deuteronomy 28:30)

Divorce and drama in homes are curses that move from generation to generation. They leave in their wake shattered lives and broken people. When there is divorce and unfaithfulness in marriage, it can have generational impact. We must undo the curse in the Courts of Heaven that would allow the enemy the right to keep propagating divorce in family lines. This devastating issue that plagues so many homes can be stopped when we recognize it to be a curse. We can see it removed and the heart of God for homes and marriages to be established.

5. A fifth trait of a curse is children being taken captive. Deuteronomy, chapter 28, verse 41, shows that children can be lost to someone or something else.

> You shall beget sons and daughters, but they shall not be yours; for they shall go into captivity. (Deuteronomy 28:41)

There is nothing as heartbreaking as watching children become captive of something else. Whether it is drugs, alcohol, gangs, sexual immorality, peer pressure, depression or other influences. This verse says they cease to be yours. In other words, the children you raised are not the ones they have become. This is because there is a curse working against them.

One of the chief things the devil wants to do is steal our children. He uses the legal right to land curses to accomplish this. If we want to bring our children out of captivity, we must remove the legal cause and right of the curse to operate. This is absolutely essential to getting children back to their destiny and what God has intended for them. Once this is done, they can move into all that God desires.

6. A sixth sign of a curse operating is no prosperity. Deuteronomy, chapter 28, verse 38, shows a lack of harvest from efforts to produce.

> You shall carry much seed out to the field but gather little in, for the locust shall consume it. (Deuteronomy 28:38)

A curse can result in no harvest from the seed you have sown. The curse can be much sowing and only a little harvest. In other words, the harvest is not commensurate to the seed that has been sown. The reason is because a devouring force eats it up. I think it's interesting that we are not talking about a supernatural harvest, but just something that should naturally occur. The sign of the curse is you don't even get what naturally should occur.

When I speak of sowing and a harvest, I am primarily speaking of what is done to make a living. Whether you own a business or work for someone else, the curse will not allow you to prosper on the level of what should naturally happen. You work hard, but the results are not equal to your labors. The answer is not more hours or even working harder. The answer is to remove the curse.

When Adam fell in the garden, the curse that came on him was one of diminished results from their labors. Genesis, chapter 3, verses 17-19, tell us that Adam would work hard, but get smaller results from his labors.

> Then to Adam He said, "Because you have heeded the voice of your wife, and have eaten from the tree of which I commanded you, saying, 'You shall not eat of it:' "Cursed is the ground for your sake; In toil you shall eat of it All the days of your life. Both thorns and thistles it shall bring forth for you, And you shall eat the herb of the field. In the sweat of your face you shall eat bread Till you return to the ground, For out of it you were taken; For dust you are, And to dust you shall return." (Genesis 3:17-19)

Adam would labor and sweat, but see thorns and thistles come, instead of great fruitfulness. This speaks of curses operating and causing a lack of prosperity, rather than fruitfulness from the labor of the hands.

In Jesus Christ this curse is removed. Yet, if we see it still operating in lives, we must move into the Courts of Heaven and take away it's legal right. When we do, the curse of lack and diminished returns is removed. The blessing of prosperity and increase is now free to come. Years of frustration and hard labor can be replaced with fruitfulness and prosperity.

7. A seventh sign of a curse operating is sicknesses that cannot be healed. Deuteronomy, chapter 28, verses 27, 35, 60-61, shows that sickness that cannot be healed are the result of a curse.

> The LORD will strike you with the boils of Egypt, with tumors, with the scab, and with the itch, from which you cannot be healed. (Deuteronomy 28:27)

> The LORD will strike you in the knees and on the legs with severe boils which cannot be healed, and from the sole of your foot to the top of your head. (Deuteronomy 28:35)

> Moreover He will bring back on you all the diseases of Egypt, of which you were afraid, and they shall cling to you. Also every sickness

and every plague, which is not written in this
Book of the Law, will the LORD bring upon
you until you are destroyed. (Deuteronomy
28:60-61)

Notice the phrase in the first two verses. It says
from "which you cannot be healed." Sicknesses that
doctors can't heal and which don't respond to prayer
for healing are a sign of a curse. There is something
legal that will not allow these diseases to be healed.
The purpose of the malady with a curse at its root is
to destroy you. The curse that is legally allowing the
disease must be removed before the sickness will leave.
There can even be an anointing that is present. It will
not have the desired effect until the curse is lifted.

When we read these verses we see that "The Lord"
is said to be afflicting with these curses. Of course, I
do not believe that "The Lord" is personally doing
this. James, chapter 1, verse 17, is very clear about The
Lord's nature.

Every good gift and every perfect gift is from
above, and comes down from the Father of
lights, with whom there is no variation or
shadow of turning. (James 1:17)

There is no darkness or even shadows in Who The Lord is. He is kind, good, compassionate and loving in all His ways. He desires only good for us. So why is the Scripture saying The Lord is bringing these curses?

We must realize as Judge, The Lord will allow the devil legally to bring destruction when he has a case against us. This is not because He desires it, but because legally He can't stop it until we deal with what is allowing it.

Hebrews, chapter 12, verse 23, shows The Lord is Judge.

> ... to the general assembly and church of the firstborn who are registered in heaven, to God the Judge of all, to the spirits of just men made perfect, ... (Hebrews 12:23)

As Judge, our God and Father, must honor the legality of the spirit realm. When Satan, as the adversary, (1 Peter 5:8) discovers a legal right to devour from, God cannot stop him. Remember the word *adversary* in 1 Peter 5:8 is the Greek word *antidikos*. It means "one who brings a lawsuit." If we do not remove the legal right of Satan, he can land curses against us to destroy with. He has a case against us that he is bringing a lawsuit from in the spirit realm.

God, as Judge, cannot stop this until we give Him the legal right to. He desires desperately to stop the ploys of Satan, but can't without the "case" against us being dealt with in the Courts of Heaven. This is the reason a curse is moving against us. A curse is always a result of a case against us in the spirit realm. The case allows the curse to light upon us. (Proverbs 26:2) It has a legal right to.

As a result of this, when the Scripture says "The Lord" is doing something evil or bad, it is looking from a large overview. It is Satan that is stealing, killing and destroying (John 10:10). It is God as Judge, Who is legally allowing it, until we take the work of Jesus on the cross and stop it.

In other words, Satan is destroying and God is HAVING TO ALLOW IT. The Lord will only allow it until we take what Jesus did on the cross, step into the Courts of Heaven, and remove the legal right of the devil. The moment this is done, The Lord moves in our behalf and Satan's rights are revoked and curses are dissolved. When we operate from a legal perspective in the Courts of Heaven, we grant God the legal right He passionately desires to move for us.

8. An eighth sign of a curse is no anointing or diminished effects of the anointing. Deuteronomy, chapter 28, verse

40, says we will not get the benefit of the anointing.

> You shall have olive trees throughout all your
> territory, but you shall not anoint yourself
> with the oil; for your olives shall drop off.
> (Deuteronomy 28:40)

Even though the source of the anointing is available, there will not be oil to anoint with. I have seen when there is a curse operating, you can pray with the anointing, sense the anointing and encounter the anointing, yet nothing will change. The reason is the curse legally has a right to stop the anointing from breaking the yoke. If we want the anointing to have its power manifested, we must deal legally with the curse. Once we take away the legal right of the curse, the anointing will bring the desired results. Yokes will be broken, sickness will be healed, deliverances will come and breakthroughs will occur.

9. A ninth sign of a curse is mental and emotional issues. Deuteronomy, chapter 28, verse 34, shows people with mental/emotional issue because of curses.

> So you shall be driven mad because of the
> sight which your eyes see. (Deuteronomy
> 28:34)

So often mental/emotional struggles can be traced to curses operating in a family line. The devil has discovered a legal place in the history of a family to cause a curse of mental illness to operate. When this history is discovered and dealt with through the blood of Jesus, the battles of mental/emotional illnesses can be won. Jesus is the One Who sets people free and delivers from torment.

10. A tenth trait of a curse is being stolen from. Deuteronomy, chapter 28, verse 31, says that the enemy will steal what is rightfully yours.

> Your ox shall be slaughtered before your eyes,
> but you shall not eat of it; your donkey shall
> be violently taken away from before you, and
> shall not be restored to you; your sheep shall
> be given to your enemies, and you shall have
> no one to rescue them. (Deuteronomy 28:31)

There is nothing more frustrating and even angering than being stolen from. Whether it is something you possessed or something that was supposed to be yours and someone else took it away, being stolen from is greatly upsetting.

This is a result of a curse that is allowing the devil a legal right to deny you what is rightfully yours. Notice also that because of this curse there is "no one to rescue them." In other words, not only do you lose it, but there is no hope of getting it back.

I know many people who have lost things— their finances, marriages, health, children, job, reputations and many other things have been ripped away from them. They keep thinking that if they just pray long enough and wait long enough that restoration will occur.

The problem is if their loss is a result of the legal right of a curse, nothing will be restored until the legal right of the curse to operate is revoked. There is a need for discernment as to what the enemy is legally using to steal their lives away. Once this is recognized, they are now ready to go "to Court" and get things in place for restoration to come. Any delay of restoration so often is not a result of the "timing of the Lord," but of still having legal issue against us in the "Courts of Heaven." The moment we get the legal issues resolved, things begin to move for our restoration to come.

As I have traveled and ministered throughout the nations, many have expressed a desire to be connected with me. They have wanted to "align" with me in the spirit realm. As they would ask about this possibility, I would always say I didn't want that responsibility toward them. It wasn't that I didn't care. It was simply that I didn't want to be distracted from the primary thing I felt called to do.

I then found myself ministering in Saskatchewan, Canada. As I finished the ministry there, the pastor/ apostle of the work had a word for me from the Lord. Without him having any knowledge of people asking me to allow them to "join" with me, he begin to prophesy it. He told me that God intended for me to do this. After this word, I went back to all those who had said they wanted to be connected with me and told them I was willing to do this.

The result was a meeting scheduled for about 30 ministries/businesses to become aligned with me. We were going to form "Global Reformers." This is the apostolic family I now lead.

About a week before this scheduled meeting, I had a dream. In the dream this meeting was going to be held at the old "Henderson home." The problem was the "home" was haunted with spirits from the past. I understood in the dream that the people who were coming to this meeting would or could be subjected to at least harassment in the spirit. I knew immediately when I awoke that I needed further cleansing of my bloodline before I allowed these precious folks to connect with me. I realized that if there were issues not dealt with in my bloodline this would cause potential attacks against those connecting with me.

We must be very cautious about how and to whom we are connected. Depending on the life of the ones who lead apostolic connections, futures can be determined. These connections in the spirit are legal in nature and allow either blessings or curses to operate. In my case, there were still things in my bloodline or Henderson house that needed to be legally dealt with.

The connecting or aligning with me in the spirit caused something legal to come into place. This would allow the devil the legal right to visit harassment, harm, oppression and other things against those connected to me. I had to cleanse my bloodline so that not only my destiny, but also the destiny of others would not be hindered. Otherwise, the devil could have a legal right to steal futures away.

I scheduled a session with a prophetic seer to help me in this process. I knew I had to do this before the meeting that initiated the function of this aligning. We, by faith, stepped into the "Courts of Heaven" and from a prophetic insight began to deal with the ghost in the Henderson home.

In other words, we dealt with anything in my bloodline that would allow the devil the legal right to not only hinder me, but those joined to me as well. The results have been awesome.

The alignment to Global Reformers that was made has helped and empowered people, ministries, ministers and businesses experience new levels of breakthroughs. The testimony of those who are a part have been that they operate in greater dimensions of authority. They share that they see new places of breakthrough because of this alignment. This occurs because of the removal and revoking of any legal right granted the devil because of issues in my bloodline or history. We were able to revoke any and every legal right of the devil to bring curses to hinder destinies.

If we are to stop the thievery of the devil, we must remove any and all legal right he is using to land curses. Once this is done, not only does the stealing stop, but restoration can come to our dreams and God's purposes.

11. An eleventh trait of a curse is you miss promotions! Deuteronomy, chapter 28, verse 43, says others will be promoted ahead of you.

> The alien who is among you shall rise higher and higher above you, and you shall come down lower and lower. (Deuteronomy 28:43)

Whether it is in business, government, church or other realms, God needs His people to succeed. He wants and needs His people in places of influence. Yet, so often, others get the promotions, instead of God's own. The reason for this is curses. The enemy uses the legal right of curses to keep God's people out of places of importance and influence. We must deal with the legal issues before the Courts of Heaven that are being used to deny and delay these places of influence.

Daniel was a man who was granted a great place of influence in Babylon. Daniel, chapter 6, verses 3-5, shows how those who were against Daniel sought a charge or case against him to stop him from being promoted.

> Then this Daniel distinguished himself above the governors and satraps, because an excellent spirit was in him; and the king gave thought to setting him over the whole realm. So the governors and satraps sought to find some charge against Daniel concerning the kingdom; but they could find no charge or fault, because he was faithful; nor was there any error or fault found in him. Then these men said, "We shall not find any charge against this Daniel unless we find it against

him concerning the law of his God." (Daniel 6:3-5)

There were those who were looking for a reason to bring a charge against Daniel to stop his promotion. They could find none. Wow! I pray, "Lord, let that be me." They could not find anything to resist him with so they convinced King Darius to set in place an edict to forbid anyone from seeking any God. Of course, Daniel did not let this stop him. The result was he was thrown into the lion's den, and God delivered him.

My main point is that the devil and his forces will use cases and charges against us to seek to deny us promotions we should have. As these cases are answered in the Courts of Heaven, promotions will come to those God has greatly loved.

12. The last trait I will mention of a curse is it causes prayers to not be answered. Deuteronomy, chapter 28, verse 23, says the heavens will be as brass and the earth as iron.

And your heavens which are over your head shall be bronze, and the earth which is under you shall be iron. (Deuteronomy 28:23)

I realize this is also talking about a literal rain not falling on the earth. It also can be applied to the spirit realm. When there is a curse operating against us, prayers that should be answered seem to go unnoticed.

Again we see this in 2 Samuel, chapter 21, verse 14, where God is said to have heeded the prayers for the land.

> They buried the bones of Saul and Jonathan his son in the country of Benjamin in Zelah, in the tomb of Kish his father. So they performed all that the king commanded. And after that God heeded the prayer for the land. (2 Samuel 21:14)

This is the account where David "fixes" the broken covenant with the Gibeonites that Saul had violated. This was what was causing the land to be in a famine and for there to be no rain.

The other part of the story is David commanded the bones of Saul and Jonathan to be put into their proper burial place. This was an act of honor toward those who had been the anointed of the Lord and David's own covenant. Through repairing the covenant with the Gibeonites and walking in a spirit of honor toward his predecessors and those he was in covenant with

(Jonathan), it moved things in the spirit realm.

The result was God heeded the prayer for the land and the famine was broken. The issue of honoring covenant is a huge thing to having issues legally in place. The result will be famines removed and prayers answered.

Anytime we are praying prayers that are in agreement with God and His word, yet they go unanswered for an extended time, something legal is resisting us. A curse has found a legal right to land against us. Once the rights of the curse are lifted and revoked, prayers will be answered and the heavens will be opened.

The earth will soften as the influence of Heaven begins to touch it. When the heavens open and are no longer brass, the earth will be softened with the rain of His grace. Our prayers begin to touch Heaven, which in turn touches earth. Curses legal right to land must be revoked. When an abundance of prayers begin to be answered, the favor of God comes to the earth.

My prayer is that we may discern the operation of any and all curses. May we not just accept things as naturally normal when they are being caused and allowed by curses legally operating against us. Once we recognize the curses operation, we will move to remove them.

How to move to remove these restricting curses will be taught in the following chapters.

CHAPTER 5

BUILDING CASES TO LAND CURSES

As I have previously stated, curses are the result of legal issues against us. We have already looked at sin, transgression and iniquity, but will review these in more detail in a later chapter. However, in this chapter, it is important for you to see how the adversary actually gathers the evidence and builds cases against us and discovers the legal right to present them.

We see in the case of Balaak hiring Balaam to curse the children of Israel that there was a searching that took place. We must know that the devil is not omniscient, omnipresent or omnipotent—only God is. However, the devil does have an extremely, well-organized legal team. He not only has those who can build cases against us, but also an investigative team that digs up information and evidence against us. Just like a legal team in the natural employs private investigators, so Satan has his as well. Their demonic responsibility is to uncover anything that can be used to build cases against us for curses to land. This is primarily done through searching our bloodlines.

When someone becomes a threat to Satan and his agenda in the earth there is a commissioning of demonic powers to search bloodlines. The purpose is to build cases, to take you to court, to gain the legal right to stop you from getting what is in your book. When you begin to flesh out what was written in your book, you will advance the Kingdom of God. (Psalm 139:16) Your Adversary, the devil knows this. His chosen method to stop you is to build a legal case against you.

Remember, this is what he did against Peter. Luke, chapter 22, verse 31, says that Satan desired or asked to have Peter.

> And the Lord said, "Simon, Simon! Indeed, Satan has asked for you, that he may sift you as wheat. But I have prayed for you, that your faith should not fail; and when you have returned to Me, strengthen your brethren." (Luke 22:31)

The word *asked* is the Greek word *exaiteomai,* and it means to demand for trial. Satan had come to an understanding of what was in Peter's book. He demanded a trial date to deny Peter what was his God-ordained destiny. Peter didn't even know anything was happening.

This is often true of us. All we know is we feel frustrated, unfulfilled and dissatisfied. The problem is there is a case against us in the Courts of Heaven, denying us what is rightfully ours.

Jesus went not as God, but as man into the Courts of Heaven. He had not yet won His place as the High Priest and/or Intercessor. When He prayed and pleaded the case for Peter, He did it as a man. This is important. If Jesus had done it as God, it would mean that we couldn't do it because we aren't God. But if He did it as a man on assignment from God, then we can also step into that dimension and function there. Jesus won the Court case on behalf of Peter and secured the destiny written in the books of Heaven concerning him.

The reason Satan took Peter to Court was because he wanted to deny him and stop him from stepping into his place of function. He knew Peter would become a massive threat to the satanic agenda in the earth. Anytime we begin to step toward what is in our book, the devil will commission his investigative team to look for evidence against us. They are assigned to search out until they find a legal reason to land curses against us—all designed to stop our destinies. This is why you always see Satan either when he was Lucifer in God's Heaven or after he was thrown out walking about.

Ezekiel, chapter 28, verse 14, shows him as Lucifer, functioning in Heaven on God's behalf.

> You were the anointed cherub who covers; I established you; You were on the holy mountain of God; You walked back and forth in the midst of fiery stones. (Ezekiel 28:14)

The fiery stones speak of a portion of the Courts of Heaven. His walking back and forth speak of his investigative purpose of building cases in and for the Courts of Heaven. Satan knows the system and how to operate in it. We can fast forward to Job, chapter 1, verse 6-8, and see that Lucifer, now as Satan after being cast out of Heaven, is still doing the same thing.

> Now there was a day when the sons of God came to present themselves before the LORD, and Satan also came among them. And the LORD said to Satan, "From where do you come?" So Satan answered the LORD and said, "From going to and fro on the earth, and from walking back and forth on it." Then the LORD said to Satan, "Have you considered My servant Job, that there is none like him on the earth, a blameless and upright man, one who fears God and shuns evil?" (Job 1:6-8)

Satan is still going to and fro and back and forth. Now he is searching to build cases against the purposes of God in the earth. Satan's purposes for going back and forth and to and fro is to gather evidence to accuse those he can in the Courts of Heaven to land curses. This is exactly what he did to Job. God points out Job, and Satan brings a case against him concerning the motives of his heart. He tells God that Job is only serving Him because He has hedged him in or there is a restraining order to stop Satan from touching him.

Job, chapter 1, verse 9-12 shows the legal wrestling that

is going on between Satan and God concerning Job.

> So Satan answered the LORD and said, "Does
> Job fear God for nothing? Have You not made
> a hedge around him, around his household,
> and around all that he has on every side?
> You have blessed the work of his hands, and
> his possessions have increased in the land.
> But now, stretch out Your hand and touch all
> that he has, and he will surely curse You to Your
> face!" And the LORD said to Satan, "Behold, all
> that he has is in your power; only do not lay a
> hand on his person." So Satan went out from the
> presence of the LORD. (Job 1:9-12)

The word *hedge* which is *swuk* in Hebrew, among other things, means to restrain. Satan is complaining that God has a restraining order against him to stop him from touching Job and what belongs to Job.

I believe that is true for us as well. Satan cannot touch us without the restraining order of God being lifted. Yet Satan brings an accusation against Job—accusing him of wrong motives. The result is God partially removes the restraining order, and Satan is allowed to trouble Job. Why was Satan's case so successful against Job? The reason might surprise us.

To see what made Satan's accusation so successful

against Job we must look at Job's offerings. Job, chapter 1, verses 4-5, unveil the motives connected to Job's offerings.

> And his sons would go and feast in their houses, each on his appointed day, and would send and invite their three sisters to eat and drink with them. So it was, when the days of feasting had run their course, that Job would send and sanctify them, and he would rise early in the morning and offer burnt offerings according to the number of them all. For Job said, "It may be that my sons have sinned and cursed God in their hearts." Thus Job did regularly. (Job 1:4-5)

The purpose of Job's offering was to deal with anything his children did against God during their partying. The offerings were not out of love and worship to and for the Lord. They were to manipulate the spirit realm and perhaps even God to be merciful. To really understand this I want to repeat what I wrote in *Operating In The Courts Of Heaven.*

In Hebrews, chapter 7, verse 8, we see that our finances and our offerings release a "witness" in Heaven.

> Here mortal men receive tithes, but there he receives them, of whom it is witnessed that he lives. (Hebrews 7:8)

The tithe, and I believe other types of offerings, give witness. The word *witnessed* is the Greek word *martureo* and it means to be a witness judicially. So our money has a voice in The Courts of Heaven. Jesus then says in Matthew, chapter 5, verses 23-26, that we must make sure our heart is right before we bring our offerings.

> Therefore if you bring your gift to the altar, and there remember that your brother has something against you, leave your gift there before the altar, and go your way. First be reconciled to your brother, and then come and offer your gift. Agree with your adversary quickly, while you are on the way with him, lest your adversary deliver you to the judge, the judge hand you over to the officer, and you be thrown into prison. Assuredly, I say to you, you will by no means get out of there till you have paid the last penny. (Matthew 5:23-26)

Jesus said if we bring our offering and remember that there is something wrong between us and another person, we must leave our offering and go get it right. Notice that Jesus didn't say this was a reason not to give our offering. He said just don't give it until your heart is fixed. Then he expounds on why we shouldn't give our offering with something wrong in our heart. He says if we do, our adversary (yes, this is the Greek word *antidikos*) will now have a case against us. We can be found guilty, thrown in prison and not get out. Our money carries the sound of our heart into the Courts of Heaven. A wrong sound or testimony from our money can give the adversary the right to bring a case against us.

This is what happened to Job. Based on the motive of his heart to manipulate God to not judge his children for their unrighteous ways, Satan could bring an accusation against Job. Satan called Job into question, concerning the motives of his heart and why he served God. Satan took the sound attached to Job's money and used it to bring a case against him.

We must make sure our offerings are given from a pure heart, out of worship and a passion for the Lord. This is why in Malachi, chapter 3, verse 3-5, we are told that God will purify our hearts for giving.

> He will sit as a refiner and a purifier of silver; He will purify the sons of Levi, And purge them as gold and silver, That they may offer to the LORD An offering in righteousness. "Then the offering of Judah and Jerusalem Will be pleasant to the LORD, As in the days of old, As in former years. And I will come near you for judgment; I will be a swift witness Against sorcerers, Against adulterers, Against perjurers, Against those who

exploit wage earners and widows and orphans,
And against those who turn away an alien—
Because they do not fear Me," Says the LORD of
hosts. (Malachi 3:3-5)

The Lord will purify us so our money has a right
testimony. Notice, this allows the Lord the right to judge
evil works in the earth. He judges sorcery, adultery, perjury,
economic inequality and more. When we, as God's people,
bring an offering in righteousness, it says the right things.
The testimony of our offering grants God the right to remove
curses from the earth that are operating. Money has a testimony
attached to it. May we make sure it is saying the right things in
the Courts of Heaven.

Now back to the issue of Balak and Balaam. Balak
the king of Midian hires Balaam to curse Israel. Balak says
to Balaam that he recognizes the great authority he carries in
the spirit. Numbers, chapter 22, verse 6, shows the power of
Balaam's words.

Therefore please come at once, curse this people
for me, for they are too mighty for me. Perhaps
I shall be able to defeat them and drive them out
of the land, for I know that he whom you bless
is blessed, and he whom you curse is cursed."
(Numbers 22:6)

For whatever reason, Balaam has a realm of authority and Balak knows it. He wants him to curse Israel so they can be weakened and then defeated. Again, this is one of the purposes of a curse. The other thing I want us to see is Balak was aware of the power of the words of one who has authority in the spirit realm. Word curses spoken by those in authority can carry great consequences.

We see this is Joshua, speaking a curse over the city of Jericho. In Joshua, chapter 6, verse 26, records the words of the curse Joshua spoke.

> Then Joshua charged them at that time, saying, "Cursed be the man before the LORD who rises up and builds this city Jericho; he shall lay its foundation with his firstborn, and with his youngest he shall set up its gates." (Joshua 6:26)

The results of this curse, in fact, was the man, Heil, who rebuilt the city—in the days of Ahab. Both of Heil's sons died as the result of Joshua's words. (1 Kings 16:34) We also see, as was previously written, that this curse on children dying continued to operate over Jericho all the ways to the days of Elisha. (2 Kings 2:19-22) Elisha then removed this curse and its operation. The thing that brought this curse was the words of Joshua.

Several years ago I had a dream where I was told that the main problem in cities and nations were not the heathen. The main problem, empowering principalities over these realms, was the men and women of God who had misused their authority God had granted them. They had spoken things and done things from the realm of authority that were granted by God that the devil now used to build cases in the Courts of Heaven. The result was curses working against what God didn't want cursed.

To understand this we must know that the accuser takes the words of those who have spiritual authority and presents them before the Courts of Heaven. He basically says to God, "These you have given authority to say this about this thing or person." He uses the words of those with spiritual authority as a legal right to bring curses. This is why those who truly carry spiritual authority must learn to use that authority correctly. They must be measured and under His authority fully. The Apostle Paul addressed this when he spoke of using his authority correctly. In 2 Corinthians, chapter 10, verse 8, tells us that authority can be used right or wrong.

> For even if I should boast somewhat more about our authority, which the Lord gave us for edification and not for your destruction, I shall not be ashamed: (2 Corinthians 10:8)

Paul said his authority was for edification, to build up not for destruction, to tear down. People who carry real spiritual authority must be careful of their words. I use to laugh at the idea that someone could "curse" me. I knew that a very high profile person had decided they didn't like me. They had believed things that were not true. This person and others who carried spiritual authority begin to speak evil of me. I again, laughed at this until ... my life began to fall apart. Then I begin to realize that their words were empowering the accuser against me with a legal right to curse me. The Lord instructed me to use Isaiah, chapter 54, verse 17.

> No weapon formed against you shall prosper, And every tongue which rises against you in judgment You shall condemn. This is the heritage of the servants of the LORD, And their righteousness is from Me," Says the LORD. (Isaiah 54:17)

This verse says several things. The first thing I want to point out is it speaks of tongues of judgment. The word *judgment* is the Hebrew word *mishpat* and it means a verdict pronounced judicially. So people's words about us can become sentences for our lives.

In other words, their words can fashion and form our destiny, rather than what God wrote in the books of Heaven. This is how powerful they can be and should not be laughed at and disregarded. We are told however that our heritage or birthright is to condemn or undo these words—literally to disturb their purpose. We can do this because His righteousness allows us to stand in the judicial place of His Courts in Heaven.

Once I saw this, I understood I needed to do four things to undo the words of those who carry spiritual authority.

First, I had to repent for all the places I have spoken critically about others with no redemptive purpose. I cannot ask for negative words about me to be undone when I am guilty of speaking negative words about others.

The second thing I did in the Courts of Heaven was I forgave those who spoke these words. The Scripture is clear that I cannot be forgiven and justified if I don't forgive others. (Luke 11:4) I had to be willing and empowered to forgive these people. As I forgave them, I asked the Lord to bless them, their family, their children, their future, their ministries and their businesses. When you really forgive, you now wish no harm or hurt to come to them—only blessings.

The third thing was I spoke off of myself the words they had spoken. I asked in the Courts of Heaven that every word that the accuser was using to bring a case against me would be annulled. I asked that these words would be stricken from the records of the Court because they are not in agreement with God's heart toward me. At this point, anything I am guilty of that they have accused me of, I need to repent. I cannot ask the Court to justify me, if I am guilty of the accusation and have not repented.

This may mean that you have to bring restitution or whatever is necessary in agreement with God's Word. There have been times when I have been dealing with significant accusations against me that I have had to make my case. For instance, I have been before the Courts of Heaven and known that someone was accusing me of stealing something from them. Not material things, but issues of the spirit. I had to make my case before the Courts and call into remembrance certain issues. As I have done this, the Court has justified me and rendered me blameless. It required a little more in depth wrestling in the Court, but the accusations against me that would have resulted in a curse were removed.

The fourth and final thing is to begin to declare your destiny as it is written in the books of Heaven. As you do this, you are replacing the verdict of their words with the destiny of God for your life. Word curses are real. This is especially true for those that are spoken by ones who carry spiritual authority.

One more short story to emphasize word curses when spoken by those who carry authority with God. We were praying over a certain part of the nation of America. A certain section of our nation was under severe drought. In fact, what had been a lush garden now looked like a desert. Every time I would fly into this location my heart would grieve over the drought and the conditions it had caused. As the network that I lead was meeting, I suddenly saw this section of our nation. I sensed clearly that God wanted us to step into the Courts of Heaven and deal with whatever was locking up the atmosphere that was not allowing it to rain.

As we begin to pray, seers and prophetic people began to hear and see a word of judgment that had been prophesied over this part of our nation. We began to repent for these words of judgment from the mouth of even real prophets. We then began to speak the word of restoration. The result was it has begun to rain and is continuing to rain. The key was to deal with the word curses that the accuser was using to shut the heavens. He was taking the words of those God has truly given spiritual authority to and using them to bring curses in the earth. We must be very careful and measured when we carry realms of authority. The adversary will use it to work against God's purposes.

Again, our New Testament mandate is Romans, chapter 12, verse 14. We are called to bless and not curse.

> Bless those who persecute you; bless and do not
> curse. (Romans 12:14)

We are set to give God the legal right to bless. We are here to lift and dissolve curses, not enact them. When we understand this, we are ready to move into the Courts of Heaven and unlock destinies.

Now back to Balaam and his efforts to curse Israel. When Balaam was called to curse Israel, Balak took him to a certain location to show him their tribes. Numbers, chapter 22, verse 41, records this positioning.

> So it was the next day, that Balak took Balaam and brought him up to the high places of Baal, that from there he might observe the extent of the people. (Numbers 22:41)

When Balak was seeking to position Balaam to curse Israel, he brought him to a place where he could see the whole of the people. We know that from that "viewpoint" he couldn't curse. He only could speak blessing. The lesson is clear though. Balaam was looking for something negative in the spirit. He couldn't just speak a curse. He had to attach it to something of a fault, failure or negative thing in Israel. He found none, and God only caused him to speak blessings.

The result was Balak moved Balaam to another place and/or angle from which he could see Israel. Numbers, chapter 23, verses 13-14, shows Balak repositioning Balaam in another place.

> Then Balak said to him, "Please come with me to another place from which you may see them; you shall see only the outer part of them, and shall not see them all; curse them for me from there." So he brought him to the field of Zophim, to the top

> of Pisgah, and built seven altars, and offered a
> bull and a ram on each altar. (Numbers 23:13-14)

Balak take Balaam to a different place and angle to look at Israel. Again, he is looking for something that will give him a legal right in the spirit to curse. He finds none and ends up blessing again. A curse has to have a legal right to land. Without it, it has no power. Balaam is looking for this.

Balak then takes him to another place or angle at which to look at Israel. Numbers, chapter 23, verses 27-28, shows Balaam being repositioned a final time.

> Then Balak said to Balaam, "Please come, I will
> take you to another place; perhaps it will please
> God that you may curse them for me from there."
> So Balak took Balaam to the top of Peor, that
> overlooks the wasteland. (Numbers 23:27-28)

Balaam is positioned to overlook the wasteland, but is still unable to curse them. Balaam can see nothing in the spirit concerning Israel that will allow him to curse them. This does, however, paint a picture of the legal strategy of the devil. He will look from every angle and every dimension to seek to find a way to curse us. He searches us out with great scrutiny. Notice what Balaam did when he found no place to curse Israel. He created one.

Revelation, chapter 2, verse 14, reveals Balaam counseled Balak on how to get a curse against Israel.

> But I have a few things against you, because you have there those who hold the doctrine of Balaam, who taught Balak to put a stumbling block before the children of Israel, to eat things sacrificed to idols, and to commit sexual immorality. (Revelation 2:14)

Balaam's counsel to Balak was to get them to eat things that were sacrificed to idols and to commit fornication. Balak tempted Israel in these areas, and they gave in. The result was a place for the curse to land. Numbers, chapter 25, verses 1-3, shows the compromise that was made that resulted in a curse and a plague.

> Now Israel remained in Acacia Grove, and the people began to commit harlotry with the women of Moab. They invited the people to the sacrifices of their gods, and the people ate and bowed down to their gods. So Israel was joined to Baal of Peor, and the anger of the LORD was aroused against Israel. (Numbers 25:1-3)

The adversary, the devil, is always looking for the legal right to land a curse. If he can't find one, he will create one through tempting us. This is what happened to Israel. Balaam knew that if Israel would compromise itself, the curse would land without his help. Numbers, chapter 25, verse 9, shows the great judgment that came from the sin of the people.

> And those who died in the plague were twenty-four thousand. (Numbers 25:9)

Twenty-four thousand died as a result of the idolatry and immorality. The devil had a legal right to bring destruction. Remember, 1 Peter, chapter 5, verse 8. He is seeking a legal right to devour. May we walk before the Lord in holiness, so his rights are revoked and we move into the destiny God has for us!

CHAPTER 6

THE ACCUSER'S PLACE

We must realize first and foremost that the devil has lost his position in the Courts of Heaven. Revelation, chapter 12, verse 10, says he has been cast down.

> Then I heard a loud voice saying in heaven, "Now salvation, and strength, and the kingdom of our God, and the power of His Christ have come, for the accuser of our brethren, who accused them before our God day and night, has been cast down." (Revelation 12:10)

We know that Satan has been cast down several times. We know he tried to ascend above God and take His place. The result was God judged him and brought him down. Isaiah, chapter 14, verses 12-15, declares the fall that occurred.

> How you are fallen from heaven, O Lucifer, son of the morning! How you are cut down to the ground, You who weakened the nations! For you have said in your heart: "I will ascend

into heaven, I will exalt my throne above the stars of God; I will also sit on the mount of the congregation On the farthest sides of the north; I will ascend above the heights of the clouds, I will be like the Most High." Yet you shall be brought down to Sheol, To the lowest depths of the Pit. (Isaiah 14:12-15)

Satan, when he was in heaven and known as Lucifer, was cast out because of his arrogance and pride to be like "The Most High." His rebellion caused him to lose his place in the "Courts of Heaven." This was not the last time he would be cast down. In the Garden of Eden when he came as the serpent and deceived and tempted Adam and Eve, his judgment was another "falling." Genesis, chapter 3, verse 14-15, shows this judgment against the serpent/devil.

So the LORD God said to the serpent: "Because you have done this, You are cursed more than all cattle, And more than every beast of the field; On your belly you shall go, And you shall eat dust All the days of your life. And I will put enmity Between you and the woman, And between your seed and her Seed; He shall bruise your head, And you shall bruise His heel." (Genesis 3:14-15)

Whatever the devil's stature was before he tempted Adam and Eve, it was reduced as a result. He clearly went from standing upright and was reduced to crawling on his belly. He was put into this position so "The Seed" would crush his head. Satan has been on a downward spiral since the day he rebelled against God.

Later, Jesus would declare that He saw Satan fall as lightning from Heaven. Luke, chapter 10, verses 17-19, says Jesus saw the downfall of Satan.

> Then the seventy returned with joy, saying, "Lord, even the demons are subject to us in Your name." And He said to them, "I saw Satan fall like lightning from heaven. Behold, I give you the authority to trample on serpents and scorpions, and over all the power of the enemy, and nothing shall by any means hurt you." (Luke 10:17-19)

When the seventy came back that Jesus had sent out to preach, heal and proclaim the Kingdom of God, they were rejoicing. They had seen the power they had in the Name of Jesus. Jesus explained this by talking about Satan falling like lightning from Heaven to earth. This was either Jesus speaking of when Satan was cast from Heaven into the earth in the beginning or something that transpired when the seventy began to preach in the Name of Jesus. I believe both ideas are appropriate.

The seventy could speak in Jesus' Name and demons obeyed because they knew Who He was. Also, when Jesus began to multiply His efforts through sending the seventy, there was a wider dethroning of Satan that was occurring.

As more and more begin to carry the authority of the Lord into the earth, Satan loses more and more of his influence and authority. In any case, Satan continues to be lowered, more and more.

Even at the end, Satan will be reduced again and again. Revelation, chapter 20, verse 1-3, shows Satan being thrown into a bottomless pit for one thousand years.

> Then I saw an angel coming down from heaven, having the key to the bottomless pit and a great chain in his hand. He laid hold of the dragon, that serpent of old, who is the Devil and Satan, and bound him for a thousand years; and he cast him into the bottomless pit, and shut him up, and set a seal on him, so that he should deceive the nations no more till the thousand years were finished. But after these things he must be released for a little while. (Revelation 20:1-3)

During the millennial reign of Christ on the earth, Satan will be bound and shut up in the bottomless pit. His influence will no longer be felt in the earth. This is another casting down that will take place. The Scripture says he will be let out of that bottomless pit for a short season. (Revelation 20:7-8) This will be allowed for one final "casting down" that will occur. When He is let out of his prison, he will begin again to deceive the nations. This is allowed, but only so he can in finality be judged and "cast down" forever. Revelation, chapter 20, verse 9-10, declares this final judgment.

> They went up on the breadth of the earth and surrounded the camp of the saints and the beloved city. And fire came down from God out of heaven and devoured them. The devil, who deceived them, was cast into the lake of fire and brimstone where the beast and the false prophet are. And they will be tormented day and night forever and ever. (Revelation 20:9-10)

The devil will be "cast" into the lake of fire and brimstone and tormented forever and ever. His judgment will be complete for his attempt at insurrection against the authority of God.

I have walked through this scenario to show that not only has Satan been cast down, but will continue to be cast down until his final judgment. Presently, Satan is operating from a cast-down place. Satan, in the beginning, occupied a position in the third Heaven. This is the place of God's Throne. It is the place of "The Courts of Heaven." Paul spoke of this dimension in 2 Corinthians, chapter 12, verses 2-4.

> I know a man in Christ who fourteen years ago—
> whether in the body I do not know, or whether
> out of the body I do not know, God knows—such
> a one was caught up to the third heaven. And I
> know such a man—whether in the body or out of
> the body I do not know, God knows—how he was
> caught up into Paradise and heard inexpressible
> words, which it is not lawful for a man to utter. (2
> Corinthians 12:2-4)

Most people believe Paul was speaking of his own experience of going to Heaven. In this place he was at a loss for words. There were no words available to describe what he saw and experienced. He couldn't even tell if he was in his body or out of his body. All he knew was he saw the third Heaven.

If there is a third Heaven, then that means there is a first and second Heaven. The Bible consistently speaks not of just Heaven, but the Heavens. Genesis, chapter 2, verse 1, declares God finished making the earth and the "Heavens."

> Thus the heavens and the earth, and all the host
> of them, were finished. (Genesis 2:1)

The "Heavens" speak of at least two dimensions that

were created. This has to be true for it to be Heavens and not Heaven. So Heavens must speak of the atmospheres above the earth. It appears that the first Heaven is the sky or atmosphere that determines the climate of the earth. In 2 Chronicles, chapter 7, verse 13, it speaks of the Heaven being shut up so it doesn't rain.

> When I shut up heaven and there is no rain ... (2 Chronicles 7:13)

Clearly the first Heaven is the atmosphere above the earth where rain forms and moisture is in the air. The second Heaven is the unseen realm that Paul spoke of in Ephesians, chapter 6, verse 12. It is here that principalities reside. It is where they lodged, when God threw the devil and his forces out of the third Heaven.

> For we do not wrestle against flesh and blood, but against principalities, against powers, against the rulers of the darkness of this age, against spiritual hosts of wickedness in the heavenly places. (Ephesians 6:12)

Notice the term "heavenly places." This speaks of another dimension of the spirit realm, or the second Heaven. All the demonic hierarchy occupy this second dimension. I have gone through the process of showing these dimensions for the purpose of stating that Satan does not dwell in the third Heaven any longer—The Throne room of God or the Courts of Heaven.

If this is true, then we should ask, "How does Satan have a right to present cases against us in this Court?" God's Court is in the third Heaven and Satan and his forces are in the second Heaven. This is a very good question. I have two answers to it.

Satan can only present a case against us if he is summoned to the Courts. We see this is Job, chapter 1, verses 6-8.

> Now there was a day when the sons of God came to present themselves before the LORD, and Satan also came among them. And the LORD said to Satan, "From where do you come?" So Satan answered the LORD and said, "From going to and fro on the earth, and from walking back and forth on it." Then the LORD said to Satan, "Have you considered My servant Job, that there is none like him on the earth, a blameless and upright man, one who fears God and shuns evil?" (Job 1:6-8)

Satan came into the Courts of Heaven because he clearly was summoned to appear. The term "sons of God" means all the created being, both angelic and demonic. Satan came among them because he is one of them and was summoned to appear. He had to give an account of himself to God, the Judge. He was allowed to be there only because he had been summoned there.

In America we know what it is to get a summons to appear in court. Whether we are being sued, a criminal case is against us, or we are being solicited to sit on a jury. If you do not show up, you are considered "FTA" or failure to appear. You have disregarded the summons and can even have an arrest warrant issued for you. You are insulting the court and making a statement against the court. Whether in the natural or in the spiritual, a summons must be honored. We must show up. This is what is happening here. So Satan was allowed to come into the Court because God summoned him and the other created beings.

While he was there, God ask Satan if he had a case against Job. This is what allowed Satan to bring his accusations. God used the accusations of one who already pleased Him to purify him to another level. Even though Job was pleasing to God, the Lord allowed a Court case against Job to perfect him and make him an overcomer. When Job went through all he did, because of the accusations of the devil, he came out an overcomer.

There are great rewards for those who overcome. Revelation, chapter 3, verse 21, speaks of just one of the rewards of being an overcomer.

> To him who overcomes I will grant to sit with Me
> on My throne, as I also overcame and sat down
> with My Father on His throne. (Revelation 3:21)

Great rewards are given to those who overcome. The problem is we must move through adverse places and even accusations of the accuser to win this place. But when we maneuver in the Courts of Heaven and qualify, we get the rewards of an overcomer. Job ended up purified, so God could trust him with double of everything he lost. God's purposes and ways are unsearchable.

Romans, chapter 11, verse 33, reveals that as much as we know about God and His ways, there are still things we don't know.

> Oh, the depth of the riches both of the wisdom
> and knowledge of God! How unsearchable are
> His judgments and His ways past finding out!
> (Romans 11:33)

Everything does indeed work together for the good of those who love God and are called according to His purpose. (Romans 8:28) As we walk through the Court process, everything intended for us by God becomes ours. This is what happened to Job as a result of his Court case.

The other thing that allows Satan to come into the Courts of Heaven is he requested or asked permission. We find this in Luke, chapter 22, verse 31. Satan asked permission to bring a case against Peter.

> And the Lord said, "Simon, Simon! Indeed, Satan
> has asked for you, that he may sift you as wheat.
> (Luke 22:31)

As I have shared previously, the word *asked* is the Greek word *exaiteomai*, which means to demand for trial, to desire. Satan had built a case against Peter and was demanding and desiring a trial date to be set against him. He couldn't just bring a case; he had to be granted the right to bring one.

This is the way our judicial system in America works as well. After someone is charged with a crime, there has to be enough evidence to warrant a trial. A "Grand Jury" is convened to examine the evidence to thoroughly determine if it warrants a trial. This "Grand Jury," if they feel that there is sufficient evidence, can then "indict" the individual. This means to formally accuse or charge with a crime.

Satan, in this scenario, is declaring that he has evidence to disqualify Peter from what in in his book or his destiny. He is declaring that he has evidence that will disqualify Peter from fulfilling what was planned for him in Heaven. Satan is appealing to God for a trial date and time to bring these charges and evidence against Peter.

The question many have is why would God allow a case to be presented by Satan against us? In addition to it giving us the right to qualify as overcomers and get those rewards, there is a couple more. God will not allow Himself to be accused of being unjust. If Satan has a case against us and God denies him the right to present it, Satan can accuse God of unrighteousness and injustice.

The Lord will not have this. The foundation of His Throne is righteousness and justice (Psalm 97:2). His Throne is the place of judicial activity in Heaven. If Satan has a legitimate case, God will allow him to present it for the sake of His integrity. The Lord is not afraid of the devil's case against us. He knows the blood of Jesus can answer any case!

The Lord also allows it to free us from any accusation that can be used against us. The Lord allows us to judicially walk through anything that Satan is using against us. When we do this, and God, by the blood of His son justifies us, these things cannot be used against us again.

Again, in the American judicial system there is something known as "Double Jeopardy." This is a term used to describe someone who has been accused of a crime and found innocent. Even if new evidence arises they cannot be charged again with this crime, once found innocent. This would be "Double Jeopardy."

Once the Court of Heaven has justified us by the blood,

we are now innocent. The thing the devil would use to resist God's purposes, which is written in our book, cannot be used again. The Lord will allow cases to be presented against us so their power against us is forever broken!

I have been operating in the Courts of Heaven and had the devil try and make cases against me from things I have already dealt with. For instance, in my bloodline there are issues of violence. This has been a consistent accusation against me to seek to deny me my future. Individuals, who have the seer gifts, have helped me cleanse my bloodline from time to time and have consistently seen this thing used against me.

I was amazed to find when I did a historical search of my family history that in Scotland the Henderson's were violent warriors. We were stationed along the border of Scotland to keep enemies out because of how vicious we were in our warfare. This can clearly be a positive thing, in that we are defenders. It can also be a negative in that the violence attached to this nature can become a problem.

The enemy is aware of this in my bloodline and will seek to use it to deny me my rights and privileges in the Courts. The adversary has also used this to resist me from bringing cases on bigger scales dealing with cities, states and nations. He will use anything he can to stop us legally from setting things in place for God's will to be done in the earth. This is why we must cleanse our bloodline, so we can present cases in the Courts beyond just our own destinies.

I have dealt with this violence issue several times before. One of the last times I was in Court the enemy wanted to bring this issue of violence up once more. This time I asked the Lord for the record of my repentance over the violence in my bloodline to be brought forward in the Court. I knew there was a recorded scroll in Heaven that chronicled my previous repentance over this issue. This record of my repentance was enough for this accusation of violence to be dismissed. When we know how to do this, we do not become victims of "Double Jeopardy" in the Courts of Heaven.

In the next chapter we will continue to talk about the nature of the accuser and his operation against us. This is very helpful in silencing him and winning our case in the Courts of Heaven!

CHAPTER 7

THE ACCUSER'S NATURE

Once we understand how the accuser is allowed to bring cases against us, it is helpful to recognize his nature and tactics. Again, Revelation, chapter 12, verse 10, points to the fact of Satan always bringing accusations against us.

> Then I heard a loud voice saying in heaven, "Now salvation, and strength, and the kingdom of our God, and the power of His Christ have come, for the accuser of our brethren, who accused them before our God day and night, has been cast down." (Revelation 12:10)

Please be reminded that the word *Accuser* is the Greek word *katagoris*. It means one who is against you in the assembly, a complainant at law. The devil is one who works from a legal position in the spirit realm. He builds cases and brings charges against us before the Lord. The purpose of these charges is to deny our destiny. They are also to devour us when and where he can. This is corroborated in 1 Peter, chapter 5, verse 8. We are told that the devil is our Adversary.

> Be sober, be vigilant; because your adversary
> the devil walks about like a roaring lion, seeking
> whom he may devour. (1 Peter 5:8)

This word *Adversary* is again the Greek word *antidikos*. It means one who brings a lawsuit. Notice that the purpose of the lawsuit is to devour us. It is to stop us from walking in our destiny, but it also is to do us harm wherever he can. John, chapter 10, verse 10, tells us that the devil is a thief to steal away everything he can.

> The thief does not come except to steal, and
> to kill, and to destroy. I have come that they
> may have life, and that they may have it more
> abundantly. (John 10:10)

He can only do this where he can find a legal right to bring a lawsuit against us. When he discovers this in our bloodline or our own personal sin and transgression, he will not stop until we stop him in the Courts of Heaven.

It is very helpful to understand the nature and the tactics of the accuser. In 2 Corinthians, chapter 2, verse 11, it tells us we must not be unlearned about his ways.

> ... lest Satan should take advantage of us; for we
> are not ignorant of his devices.(2 Corinthians 2:11)

We are not to be ignorant of the schemes and devices employed by the devil. When we are, he garnishes an advantage over us. Every time I read the word "advantage," I always think of a tennis match. My twin brother and I use to play tennis in tournaments. We won some of these as well. It was a lot of fun in our early, adult years. In playing tennis, when it is a tied score in a game, whoever wins the next point has the "advantage." This means that if they win the next point, they win that game. So to have the advantage means you are potentially one shot away from victory. Your opponent, on the other hand, is at a disadvantage.

The Bible says that when we don't know the tactics of the devil we are at the disadvantage, while he has the advantage or "ad" as it is referred to in tennis. We must not be ignorant as Paul said of his devices and ways. When we are ignorant, he has a distinct advantage over us and can be close to victory.

The word *ignorant* in the Greek is *agnoeo*. It means to not know. It also means to ignore through disinclination. In other words, ignorance can be a result of not having the right knowledge. It can also be having the knowledge, but choosing to ignore it. We must know and pay attention to the ways of the devil in the legal dimension of the spirit! If we don't do this, we risk defeat and even being devoured.

One of the ways we learn the schemes and devices of the accuser is by examining his nature in human form. Whether it is people revealing the nature of God or people revealing the nature of Satan, human flesh can and does manifest these. Even Jesus said that He came to reveal His Father. John, chapter 14, verses 8-9, shows a discourse between Philip and Jesus.

> Philip said to Him, "Lord, show us the Father, and it is sufficient for us." Jesus said to him, "Have I been with you so long, and yet you have not known Me, Philip? He who has seen Me has seen the Father; so how can you say, 'Show us the Father?'" (John 14:8-9)

Jesus was astounded that Philip, and I'm sure the others, were missing this point. One of the main reasons for Jesus' coming to earth was to reveal the true nature of the Father to us. When they saw Jesus, they also were seeing the Father and His nature. God reveals Himself through flesh and blood.

Satan as the accuser is also revealed through flesh or human form. Jesus said in John, chapter 8, verse 44, that the religious leaders were revealing their father, Satan.

> You are of your father the devil, and the desires of your father you want to do. He was a murderer from the beginning, and does not stand in the truth, because there is no truth in him. When he speaks a lie, he speaks from his own resources, for he is a liar and the father of it. (John 8:44)

Jesus said they were of their father the devil. Therefore, they displayed his nature and wanted to fulfill his desires. They were manifesting him because his nature was in them. The nature of the devil/adversary/accuser is seen in human flesh. We can learn his ways and how he operates as the accuser by looking at a human's activities. We see this in John, chapter 8, verses 2-11. In this story, Jesus is thrust into a situation with an adulterous woman. The leaders are bringing accusation against her. They also intended to bring accusation against Jesus from this circumstance. This is the story.

> Now early in the morning He came again into the temple, and all the people came to Him; and He sat down and taught them. Then the scribes and Pharisees brought to Him a woman caught in adultery. And when they had set her in the midst, they said to Him, "Teacher, this woman was caught in adultery, in the very act. Now Moses, in the law, commanded us that such should be stoned. But what do You say?" This they said, testing Him, that they might have something of which to accuse Him. But Jesus stooped down and wrote on the ground with His finger, as though He did not hear. So when they continued asking Him, He raised Himself up and said to them, "He who is without sin

among you, let him throw a stone at her first." And again He stooped down and wrote on the ground. Then those who heard it, being convicted by their conscience, went out one by one, beginning with the oldest even to the last. And Jesus was left alone, and the woman standing in the midst. When Jesus had raised Himself up and saw no one but the woman, He said to her, "Woman, where are those accusers of yours? Has no one condemned you?" She said, "No one, Lord." And Jesus said to her, "Neither do I condemn you; go and sin no more." (John 8:2-11)

This is actually a court case. *The Weymouth New Testament* actually says they made her stand in the "center of the court." They were putting this woman on trial for adultery. The penalty was death, should she be found guilty. They are seeking to use this scenario to also bring an accusation against Jesus based on His answers. From this story we can discern the nature and tactics of the accuser, working through those who are under his control. We can find out some of the ways he operates so we can better defend ourselves from his accusations in court.

When the devil accuses us before God's Throne, it will always bring shame and condemnation. In fact, one of the ways you can know there is a case against you before the Courts of Heaven, is the shame you inexplicably sense and carry. This woman was caught in the very act of adultery. It is early morning, according to Scripture. She has clearly been drug out of a man's bed, probably with little or no clothes on. They have stood her in the middle of this "court" to be tried. Not only is she afraid for her life, but she is standing there in utter and complete shame, maybe even nakedness. This is the spirit of the accuser at work.

Shame is one of the most demeaning and destructive forces. Many people are living under this spirit of shame because of a case against them in the Courts of Heaven. The reason for the shame is the accusations being leveled at you in the Court. You intuitively are picking up in your spirit what the devil is saying about you in the Courts. This must be dealt with. Shame, if it is unresolved, will devour everything that is precious. Jeremiah, chapter 3, verses 24-25, declares the power of shame.

> For shame has devoured The labor of our fathers from our youth—Their flocks and their herds, Their sons and their daughters. We lie down in our shame, And our reproach covers us. For we have sinned against the LORD our God, We and our fathers, From our youth even to this day, And have not obeyed the voice of the LORD our God. (Jeremiah 3:24-25)

Notice that shame, coming even from youthful times, is devouring flocks and herds. This is the Body of Christ, the Church. The people of the Church are devoured and eaten away by shame. Destinies are lost and forfeited because of shame that is coming from the accusation of the accuser. Sons and daughters are also being devoured.

Shame is quite often used to try and motivate children. Shame is not a proper motivator. It actually fashions wrong thinking about yourself and makes you want to give up and not try. Don't use shame to motivate children or anyone else.

Also notice, "we lie down in our shame." This means there is no vision. Shame causes people to feel completely unworthy of dreaming big dreams about themselves. They simply lie down and have no motivation for greatness. This can be the result of the enemy releasing a case against us in the Courts of Heaven. We must know how to go into the Courts and repent for every place we have disobeyed the Lord. We ask for the blood of Jesus to speak for us and undo the spirit of shame and condemnation. There is freedom and dreams for the future on the other side of this Court case!

Another part of the nature and tactics we see is the accuser uses God's law and standard against us. John, chapter 8, verse 5, shows the accusers using Moses' law as their point of accusation.

Now Moses, in the law, commanded us that such
should be stoned. But what do You say? (John
8:5)

The Law of God and the standard of God we have broken
is always what's used against us to build cases and bring curses.
The accuser takes the Word of the Lord and uses it to build cases
against us. Every place we have disobeyed and transgressed His
Law, the devil documents it. This is always the basis for his
case against us. Of course this means not only our personal sin,
but the sin of our bloodline. He also builds cases against cities,
states and nations from the disobedience to God's Word within
the history of cultures.

 This is why we must repent of everything we are aware
of. When we do this, we are agreeing with the blood of Jesus
to silence and remove these accusations. Also, in this verse, we
see that the ultimate purpose of the accuser is to steal, kill and
destroy. They wanted this woman dead. They desired to stone
her and were willing to sacrifice her life to make a case against
Jesus. The purpose of cases against us in the Courts of Heaven
is to steal away dreams, kill ambition and destroy destinies. We
cannot imagine how cruel and malicious the accuser really is.
We must know how to answer every accusation to silence his
desires and secure our destinies.

 We can also see from this account that temptation is to
secure cases against us. John, chapter 8, verse 6, says they were

seeking something to accuse Jesus with. They had set up this scenario to try and trap Jesus. The real person they wanted to bring the case against wasn't even the woman—it was Jesus.

> This they said, testing Him, that they might have something of which to accuse Him. But Jesus stooped down and wrote on the ground with His finger, as though He did not hear. (John 8:6)

As with Jesus, the accuser sets traps for us. He wants to lure us into a place of sin, so he can have a legal right to destroy. When you realize this, it will propel you to greater realms of holiness. When we give in to temptation, we are actually granting the accuser evidence to build cases against us. This is why 1 John, chapter 2, verse 1, is a verse to live by.

> My little children, these things I write to you, so that you may not sin. And if anyone sins, we have an Advocate with the Father, Jesus Christ the righteous. (1 John 2:1)

The first ambition and desire should be to not sin. If we sin, however, we should be quick to repent. When we repent, Jesus Christ the righteous, our Advocate, stands on our behalf. We are forgiven based on Jesus' representation on our behalf before the Father. We must deal with things quickly, so we don't give the devil the legal right to devour. This is the purpose of temptation. It is not just to get us to sin, but to even create a legal right to devour us.

In this story we also see a revelation of who the Intercessor is and who the Accuser is. John, chapter 8, verses 10-11, shows the heart of both and them contrasted.

> When Jesus had raised Himself up and saw no one but the woman, He said to her, "Woman, where are those accusers of yours? Has no one condemned you?" She said, "No one, Lord." And Jesus said to her, "Neither do I condemn you; go and sin no more." (John 8:10-11)

The accusers purpose is to bring us under judgment and condemnation. The purpose of Jesus, Who stands as our Intercessor, is to free us from all judgment. Through this courtroom activity, the woman was freed from something the Law would have demanded. Jesus, operating as her Advocate, was able to answer accusations and set her free. Sometimes people think Jesus is standing against them. This is not true. Romans, chapter 8, verses 32-34, declares what is working on our behalf in the Courts of Heaven.

> He who did not spare His own Son, but delivered Him up for us all, how shall He not with Him

also freely give us all things? Who shall bring a charge against God's elect? It is God who justifies. Who is he who condemns? It is Christ who died, and furthermore is also risen, who is even at the right hand of God, who also makes intercession for us. (Romans 8:32-34)

These verses, among other things, declare if Jesus is resisting and condemning us—He is working against His own sacrifice. He's not condemning us; He is interceding for us in the Courts of Heaven. He is standing as the Mediator, Great High Priest and Intercessor, making intercession for us. All of Heaven is working on our behalf to answer every accusation against us. There is no charge against us that can stand as we humble our heart, repent and accept and declare His blood that was shed for us.

As Jesus was dealing with these accusers, He is seen waiting on the Holy Spirit for the answer to their accusations. They ask and keep on asking Him for His judgment. He simply kneels down in John, chapter 8, verses 6-9, and writes in the dirt.

This they said, testing Him, that they might have something of which to accuse Him. But Jesus stooped down and wrote on the ground with His finger, as though He did not hear. So when they continued asking Him, He raised Himself up and said to them, "He who is without sin among you, let him throw a stone at her first." And again He stooped down and wrote on the ground. Then those who heard it, being convicted by their conscience, went out one by one, beginning with the oldest even to the last. And Jesus was left alone, and the woman standing in the midst. (John 8:6-9)

Many people have said he wrote the names of the accusers and their sin. Perhaps, he wrote the name of the man the woman was sleeping with, which by the way wasn't on trial, even though he should have been by the standard of the law. All of this is fine. I believe He simply was waiting on the Holy Spirit to give Him the answer to the accusations. As He waited, He wrote in the dirt. When He heard the answer He spoke it. The result was mass conviction in the hearts of all the accusers. The case was dismissed, the woman freed and Jesus not trapped. This all happened because Jesus depended on and listened to the Holy Spirit.

When we are answering and making cases in the Courts of Heaven, we must listen to the Holy Spirit. Someone recently told me that after researching the word *Comforter* in the Greek, which refers to the Holy Spirit, they found it to mean "one who brings legal aid." The Holy Spirit knows how to help us answer any and every accusation in the Courts of Heaven.

I have found myself in The Courts of Heaven having to defend myself against attacks by those who carry spiritual authority. These are God's people who have decided they don't like me. This does happen, but shouldn't. They have gone into the Courts and made cases against me that is empowering demonic accusations. It has taken the wisdom of the Spirit of God to answer these cases and make my own case in the situation. To leave this undone would be to invite curses to land based on their accusations. I have had to allow the Holy Spirit to give me counsel in how to bring my own case and silence those accusations. This is what Jesus was doing. He waited on the counsel of the Spirit of God. When it came, He spoke the word that shifted everything.

Once the accusations were answered and the accusers were silenced, the Bible says they all went out. John, chapter 8, verse 9, shows them all leaving with convicted consciences.

> Then those who heard it, being convicted by their
> conscience, went out one by one, beginning with
> the oldest even to the last. And Jesus was left alone,
> and the woman standing in the midst. (John 8:9)

I have found that as we deal with the accuser in Court, when we win the case against him, he leaves. Once he leaves, we are free to ask for that which he has been resisting. The Lord is now free to answer our prayers and release to us the destinies belonging to us. This is what Jesus did with this lady. He asked her where her accusers were. They had all left. He then spoke words of life. He said, "Go and sin no more." Not only was she forgiven, but Jesus gave her life back to her because He won in Court!

What that must have felt like for this woman! Facing certain death because of her sin. She then had Jesus stand for her and free her from the accusations and judgments. She now has her life back to be filled with destiny. Jesus always has an answer to the accusations. We can go into the Courts with Him and answer every accusation because of the blood and Who Jesus is.

CHAPTER 8

REVOKING THE RIGHTS OF PRINCIPALITIES AND POWERS

I was in Hawaii teaching on dissolving curses. I had taught a few sessions and began to lead the people in prayer to undo these curses. As I was praying, it was like a veil separated, and I saw the question in the spirit realm that had to be answered. The question was, "Who do these people belong to?"

I suddenly realized that there were principalities that were claiming these people for their purposes. Not just the people in the meeting, but the whole Polynesian culture. Their debate and contention in the spirit realm was that a covenant had been made with them through blood sacrifice that had dedicated these people to them. They were unwilling to let them go, and therefore, had a right to afflict them with curses.

This applied especially to those who had turned to the Lord. It wasn't about going to Heaven. It was about getting the fullness of the Kingdom manifested in the earth now! Revelation, chapter 12, verse 10-11, is a significant Scripture in understanding this.

Then I heard a loud voice saying in heaven, "Now salvation, and strength, and the kingdom of our

God, and the power of His Christ have come, for the accuser of our brethren, who accused them before our God day and night, has been cast down. And they overcame him by the blood of the Lamb and by the word of their testimony, and they did not love their lives to the death." (Revelation 12:10-11)

The word *accuser* in the Greek is *katagoris*. It means one against you in the assembly; a complainant at law. Just like the word *Adversary* is "one who brings a lawsuit, this word *katagoris* also describes the legal position Satan and his forces hold in the Courts of Heaven—bringing complaints against us in the judicial system of Heaven. Please notice that it is these complaints that are stopping the full breakthrough and manifestation of the Kingdom of God.

John heard a voice declaring, "Now salvation, and strength, and the kingdom of our God and the power of His Christ have come." This implies that a full manifestation of the Kingdom of God is now in the earth. The problem with this is there has not been a full manifestation of the Kingdom in the earth to date. If this had occurred, all sick people in the Body of Christ would be healed. There would be no premature death. There would be reformed cities and discipled nations. This simply is not true … yet.

This means when John heard the voice saying, "Now,"

it was somewhere in the future. Of course this is consistent with the Book of Revelation because it is a futuristic book. So we are still waiting on the full and complete manifestation of Kingdom power and rule.

Notice what happens to allow this manifestation to come. It isn't a battle or war on a battlefield. It is the fact that the "accuser" the *katagoris* is silenced and his complaints and accusations are removed. The thing that is stopping a full manifestation of God's Kingdom isn't the timing of God, but the removal of the legal accusations of the devil. He still has a case against us that we must remove and deal with. When this occurs, God will be free to see a complete demonstration of Who He is in the earth. We, as His people, have a major part to play in this process.

This is what I was dealing with in Hawaii. The principalities that covenants had been made with in the Polynesian culture were still able to claim these people as their own. Even though it had been centuries since human and blood sacrifices were offered in demonic rituals, in the spirit realm, these powers will not let go. They claim to have legal rights to these people. The individuals are saved, born-again and have eternal life. Yet, as a part of the culture, the enemy has a right to resist and withstand the future God has for them.

There are two levels on which this can be dealt with. As individuals, we can go before the Courts of Heaven and cleanse our bloodline. The deeper we do this, the more the principalities must let go of our family line. Their claim to us is broken as we deal with the iniquitous patterns of our ancestry and history. I will give some practical steps in how to do this in a later chapter.

The second level we can deal with is on a cultural level. Principalities and Powers hold cultures captive based on the iniquity or sin in their bloodline. In 2 Corinthians, chapter 4, verses 3-4, tells us that people are blinded by the god of this age.

> But even if our gospel is veiled, it is veiled to those who are perishing, whose minds the god of this age has blinded, who do not believe, lest the light of the gospel of the glory of Christ, who is the image of God, should shine on them. (2 Corinthians 4:3-4)

The god of this age is a title and the name of Satan and his forces. They are blinding people and not allowing the Gospel to impact them unto salvation. This can definitely be on a personal level, but Paul is speaking more on a cultural level. He is explaining why the good news of the Gospel can be preached and the masses don't respond. It is because the god of this age has blinded them.

As with all other things, these powers of darkness cannot do this without a legal right. They must be empowered by something legal in the spirit realm to cause this blindness and dullness to the Gospel. Their empowerment is the iniquity in the culture. The devil is using the iniquitous past and history of the culture as a legal right to stop mass evangelism.

Let me explain it this way. Early in Jesus' ministry we see him reaching the "ones." Nathanael is a good example of this. John, chapter 1, verses 45-51, records Philip bringing Nathanael to Jesus.

> Philip found Nathanael and said to him, "We have found Him of whom Moses in the law, and also the prophets, wrote—Jesus of Nazareth, the son of Joseph." And Nathanael said to him, "Can anything good come out of Nazareth?" Philip said to him, "Come and see." Jesus saw Nathanael coming toward Him, and said of him, "Behold, an Israelite indeed, in whom is no deceit!" Nathanael said to Him, "How do You know me?" Jesus answered and said to him, "Before Philip called you, when you were under the fig tree, I saw you." Nathanael answered and said to Him, "Rabbi, You are the Son of God! You are the King of Israel!" Jesus answered and said to him, "Because I said to you, 'I saw you under the fig tree,' do you believe? You will see greater things than these." And He said to him, "Most assuredly, I say to you, hereafter you shall see heaven open, and the angels of God ascending and descending

upon the Son of Man." (John 1:45-51)

Jesus saw Nathanael under the "fig tree." This is significant. The fig tree spoke of Israel as a nation and the spirit that dominated Israel as a nation. Hosea, chapter 9, verse 10, verifies the fig tree being symbolic of Israel.

> I found Israel Like grapes in the wilderness; I saw your fathers As the firstfruits on the fig tree in its first season. But they went to Baal Peor, And separated themselves to that shame; They became an abomination like the thing they loved. (Hosea 9:10)

Here the prophet is likening Israel and its history to a fig tree. God is grieving because even though he had revealed Himself in Israel, they had forsaken Him for other gods. So the fig tree is symbolic of Israel and the spirit that came to control it. That spirit was a religious spirit that rejected Jesus and was threatened by Him. It is no small coincidence that one of the last things Jesus did in his earthly ministry was "curse or judge the fig tree." Mark, chapter 11, verses 13-14, shows Jesus cursing this tree.

> And seeing from afar a fig tree having leaves, He went to see if perhaps He would find something

on it. When He came to it, He found nothing but leaves, for it was not the season for figs. In response Jesus said to it, "Let no one eat fruit from you ever again." And His disciples heard it. (Mark 11:13-14)

After Jesus cursed and judged this fig tree, He then went on into the city of Jerusalem. As they returned the next day, they saw the fig tree withered away. Mark, chapter 11, verse 20, declares what Jesus had judged had withered quickly.

Now in the morning, as they passed by, they saw the fig tree dried up from the roots. (Mark 11:20)

Jesus did not just curse a literal fig tree. He judged the spirit that was dominating and controlling Israel. Jesus, up until this time, had spent his years of earthly ministry pulling "ones" out from under the fig tree. When He judged that spirit, Peter stood a few days later on the Day of Pentecost, and preached one sermon that resulted in 3,000 people being added to the Church.

Even though Jesus spoke to multitudes, He only had 120 who were committed followers and disciples. The religious spirit blinded the eyes of those who heard … lest they should see. There was no cultural impact and revival. When Jesus judged the fig tree, that which was controlling the atmosphere of a culture was broken, and they were free to respond to the good news and preaching of Peter!

If we are to see massive revival, and not just see the "ones" come to the Lord, we must deal with the god of this age that is blinding their minds. The culture has to be freed from these legally empowered principalities. When we move into the Courts of Heaven and see these power's legal rights revoked, great revivals will again shake the earth.

Zechariah, chapter 3, verses 1-9, shows Joshua, the High Priest, being qualified to stand in the Courts on behalf of a culture and a nation.

> Then he showed me Joshua the high priest standing before the Angel of the LORD, and Satan standing at his right hand to oppose him. And the LORD said to Satan, "The LORD rebuke you, Satan! The LORD who has chosen Jerusalem rebuke you! Is this not a brand plucked from the fire?" Now Joshua was clothed with filthy garments, and was standing before the Angel. Then He answered and spoke to those who stood before Him, saying, "Take away the filthy garments from him." And to him He said, "See, I have removed your iniquity from you, and I will clothe you with rich robes." And I said, "Let them put a clean turban on his head." So they put a

clean turban on his head, and they put the clothes on him. And the Angel of the LORD stood by. Then the Angel of the LORD admonished Joshua, saying, "Thus says the LORD of hosts: 'If you will walk in My ways, And if you will keep My command, Then you shall also judge My house, And likewise have charge of My courts; I will give you places to walk Among these who stand here. 'Hear, O Joshua, the high priest, You and your companions who sit before you, For they are a wondrous sign; For behold, I am bringing forth My Servant the BRANCH. For behold, the stone That I have laid before Joshua: Upon the stone are seven eyes. Behold, I will engrave its inscription,' Says the LORD of hosts, 'And I will remove the iniquity of that land in one day. In that day,' says the LORD of hosts, 'Everyone will invite his neighbor Under his vine and under his fig tree.'" (Zachariah 3:1-9)

In these verses, we see the filthiness of Joshua the High Priest. The position of High Priest is the highest office and position in the Courts of Heaven, other than God the Judge of All. Jesus now occupies this position of High Priest. From this position He has secured salvation for all who will come. He has taken His own blood and offered it. He and His blood now speak with other voices giving God the legal right to reclaim all things back to Himself. (Hebrews 12:24)

Joshua, the High Priest, was a prophetic declaration of Jesus Who was to come. Yet, he was unclean, and in the spirit, was clothed with filthy garments. We should know that we all have on certain garments in the spirit. We do not look like in the spirit what we look like in the natural. The attire we wear in the spirit speaks of our position, standing and rank in this unseen realm. This is why the priests wore a certain attire. Even though it was garments in the natural, it spoke of the spirit dimension they were called to function in.

Exodus, chapter 28, verses 2-4, gives us an overview of the priestly garments they were to wear.

> And you shall make holy garments for Aaron your brother, for glory and for beauty. So you shall speak to all who are gifted artisans, whom I have filled with the spirit of wisdom, that they may make Aaron's garments, to consecrate him, that he may minister to Me as priest. And these are the garments which they shall make: a breastplate, an ephod, a robe, a skillfully woven tunic, a turban, and a sash. So they shall make holy garments for Aaron your brother and his sons, that he may minister to Me as priest. (Exodus 28:2-4)

These garments were made so they could minister to the Lord as Priest. Wearing these garments is what qualified them to function in their priesthood. These garments were for glory and beauty. These garments consecrated them and spoke of their rank, position and function in the spirit.

Each of us also were garments that speak of our function, position and rank. We should desire the right garments to function as priest unto our God. Our job as priest unto our God is to grant God the legal right to bless and not judge. This is what the priest would do. They would offer sacrifices that granted God the legal right to show mercy, instead of releasing judgment. Whether it was the Day of Atonement, when the High Priest would go behind the veil and sprinkle and pour out the blood, or Aaron running with a censer with incense to stop the plague, the Priest always moved God to be merciful.

I cannot find a place in Scripture where the Priest brought judgment. Through the sacrifice they offered, they always gave God the right to be merciful. We are told that we are priests unto our God (1 Peter 2:9, Revelation 1:6, Revelation 5:10). So our job in the Spirit as Priest is to take the blood of Jesus and administrate it as a part of His Priesthood, so God can be legally merciful. It is the blood of Jesus that gives God the legal right to be merciful. We are granted the high and complete honor of being a part of that process.

Joshua, the High Priest, in his day is occupying the highest place in the Courts of Heaven. The problem is he is unclean. His uncleanness is a result of iniquity in his bloodline. Zechariah, chapter 3, verse 4, tells us that God purged his iniquity from him.

> Then He answered and spoke to those who stood before Him, saying, "Take away the filthy garments from him." And to him He said, "See, I have removed your iniquity from you, and I will clothe you with rich robes." (Zechariah 3:4)

There was something in Joshua's bloodline that Satan was using to make him unclean. Joshua may not have been guilty of a particular sin, but there was iniquity in his bloodline the enemy was using. Through this iniquity, Joshua was filthy in the spirit realm. He had on the right garments for function, position and rank, but they were dirty. This was prohibiting him from presenting cases in the Courts of Heaven that he, as the High Priest, could only present. Without a case being presented, nothing could be done, and Satan would win by default. God had to clean Joshua up so he could function in the spirit realm for the sake of God's purposes in the earth!

We see this same principle in Isaiah, chapter 43, verses 25-28.

> "I, even I, am He who blots out your transgressions for My own sake; And I will not remember

your sins. Put Me in remembrance; Let us contend together; State your case, that you may be acquitted. Your first father sinned, And your mediators have transgressed against Me. Therefore I will profane the princes of the sanctuary; I will give Jacob to the curse, And Israel to reproaches. (Isaiah 43:25-28)

God declares that Israel as a nation is under curses and reproach. One of the reasons is the "mediators" have transgressed. The mediators were those who had the right to present cases in the Courts of Heaven. God is declaring that He is blotting out the transgressions and remembering the sins no more. He says He is doing this for His own sake.

In other words, God needs them cleaned up and qualified to present cases in His Courts. Without them and the cases presented to grant Him the legal right to bless, Israel will continue to function under a curse. The devil will win by default because no one is found worthy to function in the Courts of Heaven. God's solution is to forgive and cleanse them for His sake. Sometimes, the greatest thing we have going for us is God needs us. He needs us as Priests to step into His Courts and present cases that can even remove curses and reproach from nations.

This is what is happening with Joshua, the High Priest. This is why God rebukes Satan away from Joshua—He had chosen Jerusalem. Zechariah, chapter 3, verse 2, shows that it was for Jerusalem's sake, not Joshua's sake, that God cleansed him.

> And the LORD said to Satan, "The LORD rebuke you, Satan! The LORD who has chosen Jerusalem rebuke you! Is this not a brand plucked from the fire?" (Zechariah 3:2)

God needed Joshua to function in his positions so that God's will and purpose could be accomplished in Jerusalem. We are necessary to the purposes of God. God needs us to take our place to remove curses from individuals all the way up to nations.

There is one final thing I want us to notice about this account. God promises that as Joshua operates in the spirit realm that the iniquity of a nation can be removed in one day. Zechariah, chapter 3, verse 9, declares something legal shifting in a nation that allows blessing and not curses to come.

> For behold, the stone That I have laid before Joshua: Upon the stone are seven eyes. "Behold, I will engrave its inscription," Says the LORD of hosts, "And I will remove the iniquity of that land in one day." (Zechariah 3:9)

Through the legal process in the Courts of Heaven, God promised to remove the iniquity of a land in one day. Sometimes, we think it is a long and enduring process to see generations of iniquity removed. God says, when we learn to go into the Courts of Heaven for a nation, we can see the legal issue of iniquity removed in a day. As the right ones, who are set by God function in the Courts of Heaven, the legal rights of the Satanic are removed. When this happens the legal right that iniquity has been giving powers of darkness over nations is revoked. The blinders will come off of people and massive revival will occur. This happens because a people called, commissioned, rightly dressed and empowered have boldly come before the Courts of Heaven. The result is curses moved off of nations and mighty moves of God are free to come!

CHAPTER 9

SECRETS TO BLOODLINE CLEANSING

If there are issues in our bloodline that we have not dealt with, Satan will use these to attack us and deny us the right to function in the Courts of Heaven. It is imperative to deal with any and all bloodline issues that we can. This is a safeguard for us, and it also allows us to function before the Courts of Heaven.

As I shared in the last chapter, Joshua, the High Priest, was resisted by Satan because of the iniquity in his bloodline. As a matter of reminder, Zechariah, chapter 3, verse 4, says God cleansed the iniquity that was making him have on unclean garments in the spirit realm.

> Then He answered and spoke to those who stood before Him, saying, "Take away the filthy garments from him." And to him He said, "See, I have removed your iniquity from you, and I will clothe you with rich robes." (Zechariah 3:4)

God graciously removed Joshua's filthy garments and gave him rich, new robes. His iniquity was cleansed, and he wore new garments in the spirit realm, which allowed his function there. We, too, must experience this. The iniquity of the bloodline must be cleansed so we can present cases in The Courts. Also, it is so often the iniquity in the bloodline that allows backlash to touch us. When we are being successful against the powers of darkness, they will look for legal rights to backlash against us. When we cleanse our bloodlines we are taking away this right.

There are several facts concerning bloodlines that we should realize. These facts will help us in the process of seeing our bloodlines cleansed. There are some secrets I have learned concerning this process. This is the most common question that arises when I teach on "The Courts of Heaven." People desire to know how to get their bloodlines cleansed and revoke any legal right of the devil to land curses against them. Here are some facts.

First of all, we must know that when Jesus died on the cross ALL our sins, transgression and iniquities were dealt with. Colossians, chapter 2, verse 14, shows this.

> … having wiped out the handwriting of requirements that was against us, which was contrary to us. And He has taken it out of the way, having nailed it to the cross. (Colossians 2:14)

This is a part of the verdict that flowed out of the cross of Jesus. Remember, that the cross was the greatest legal transaction in history. Every handwriting of requirements against us was taken out of the way. The word *handwriting* is the Greek word *cheirographon*, and it means a legal document handwritten. The word *requirement* is the Greek word *dogma* and it means a law. So every legally handwritten law that was against us, Jesus' sacrifice took it away. This is speaking of the accusations against us in the Courts of Heaven. Jesus' cross is all we need for the accusations and laws against us to be dismissed. This is the verdict that was rendered at the cross.

This verse also says that what was "contrary" to us was taken away. The word *contrary* is the Greek word *hupenantios,* and it means to be covertly contrary to. In other words, even things that are against us that are covert or hidden, Jesus' atonement dealt with these as well. This is good news. When I am dealing with my bloodline, I deal with all I know. The things I don't know, I use this legally in the Courts of Heaven. I declare, "I repent for the specific things I am aware of, but I also ask for this verdict from the Cross to cleanse the covert or hidden things in my bloodline." This is the power of Jesus' sacrifice. When we, by faith in his work for us on the Cross execute it into place, it deals with any and every accusation/ case against us in the Courts of Heaven.

The second thing we must know in regards to this is the execution of the finished works of the Cross is imperative to winning in the Courts and revoking curses. As I stated earlier in this book an unexecuted verdict has no power. This is why the devil/adversary keeps trying to use things against us. There are those who would tell us that it is automatic because Jesus died for us. If this were true then why are people still sick and dying prematurely in the Body of Christ? If what they say is true, then people should be healed the moment they accept Jesus as their Savior. The Cross clearly, legally, brought healing just like forgiveness of sins. Isaiah, chapter 53, verse 5, tells us the suffering of Jesus not only provided for the forgiveness of our sins, but also for our sicknesses.

> But He was wounded for our transgressions, He
> was bruised for our iniquities; The chastisement
> for our peace was upon Him, And by His stripes
> we are healed. (Isaiah 53:5)

This is the verdict Jesus secured through His death. That verdict, as any other verdict, has no power—unless it is executed into place. This is one of the reasons why the Holy Spirit came. He is here to empower us to execute the finished works of Jesus into full place. Again, John, chapter 16, verse 11, tells us that a judgment or verdict was rendered when Jesus died. The Holy Spirit is the One Who empowers us to execute that verdict into place.

... of judgment, because the ruler of this world is
judged. (John 16:11)

We, through the anointing and authorization of the Spirit,
take what Jesus did on the cross and silence every accusation.
We win every time in the Courts when we know how to operate
there.

There are many ways to execute the verdict into place in
the Courts. In dealing with bloodline issues though repentance
is absolutely necessary. The accuser/adversary is bringing
accusation against us; therefore, we need the blood to speak for
us. Hebrews, chapter 12, verse 24, tells us that the blood is still
speaking today.

... to Jesus the Mediator of the new covenant,
and to the blood of sprinkling that speaks better
things than that of Abel. (Hebrews 12:24)

The blood that Jesus sprinkled in the Courts of Heaven
for us is not something that has spoken. The Bible says the blood
is still speaking. Jesus' blood that He offered is still speaking to
secure our destinies and redemption. When we repent, we are
coming into agreement with what the blood of Jesus is saying
in the Courts of Heaven. We are saying, "Do not allow my sins,
transgressions and iniquities to stop the destiny written for me
in the books of Heaven. Let the blood that grants God the legal

right to forgive and bless, speak on my behalf. I humble myself before the Living God and ask that every transgression, sin and iniquity be washed away by the precious blood of the Lamb." When we do this, we are taking the finished works of Jesus on the cross and answering every accusation the accuser can use against us.

The third fact about cleansing the bloodline is in knowing our bloodlines go all the way back to Adam and Eve. Usually the Scripture found in Exodus, chapter 20, verse 5, is referred to.

> ... you shall not bow down to them nor serve them. For I, the LORD your God, am a jealous God, visiting the iniquity of the fathers on the children to the third and fourth generations of those who hate Me ... (Exodus 20:5)

Most people, who believe in bloodline cleansing, think it relates only four generations back. The problem is that the fourth generation back is connected to the previous four. Then they are connected to the next previous four, and so on. It ultimately ends up back at Adam and Eve. So when we pray and say, "I lay my life down through my father and mother all the way to Adam and Eve," we are granting the Holy Spirit the right to search out anything the enemy could use to build a case against us. I want to give the Lord full rights and privileges to search my bloodline completely.

The fourth fact is we should investigate what we can with natural knowledge. When you begin to cleanse your bloodline, you should look at your parents, you and your siblings and your children. Any additional generations such as grandparents and grandchildren can also help if you have information concerning them. As you look at these generations, you will discover iniquitous patterns.

As I have done this for myself, I discovered addictive behaviors, fear, sexual perversion, anger, violence, negligence, lack of stewardship and others. I began by repenting for these issues in my bloodline. I have discovered that when we are faithful to search out natural knowledge, God will bring supernatural knowledge.

I have a dear friend who heard my teaching on bloodline issues and the rights they grant for a curse to land. He then told me the story of many of his siblings dying at a very young age. After one of his brothers had died prematurely, his grandmother came to him. She told him a "family secret" no one knew. His grandfather in his younger years had killed a man in a bar fight with a knife. This information was not known. The grandmother knew that the string of premature deaths in the family line was connected to the killing that had been done by the grandfather. The accuser was taking occasion of this incident to legally kill the generations after the grandfather.

Genesis, chapter 9, verse 5-6, tells us the legal right the devil uses to bring premature death.

> Surely for your lifeblood I will demand a reckoning; from the hand of every beast I will require it, and from the hand of man. From the hand of every man's brother I will require the life of man. "Whoever sheds man's blood, By man his blood shall be shed; For in the image of God He made man." (Genesis 9:5-6)

When the grandfather killed that man, it gave the devil a legal right to kill other members of the family prematurely. My friend went into the Courts of Heaven on his and his family's behalf to take away that legal right. He was successful, because the blood of Jesus always wins where there is genuine repentance.

The fifth fact is we should ask the Lord for supernatural knowledge. This can come through visions and dreams. I have learned to pay very close attention to my dreams. They can and do reveal legal issues in the spirit that I need to deal with. I interpret many dreams now from a Courtroom mentality.

During the Presidential election of 2016 I dreamed that one of the candidates called me on the phone. They told me I was to hold a meeting/conference concerning the election. I knew I was to gather people together to move into the Courts of Heaven. We were to take our place and present cases in the Courts to shift things in America for God's will to be done. From the Court of Heaven, we were to present cases to revoke the rights of principalities from determining the outcome of this election. If we are going to see God's purposes done in nations, there must be a people to go to Court for the nations.

There must be those who are recognized in "The Courts" to present cases for God's will to be done. Nations hang in the balance, awaiting cases to be presented and argued in "The Courts." May we take our position in "The Courts of Heaven" and work with God to see His passion in nations fulfilled. If we will ask the Lord, He will unveil supernatural knowledge in issues of our bloodline and the bloodline of cultures that we need to deal with and process through. When this is done, even nations can be freed from curses and destinies secured.

The sixth fact in dealing with our bloodline is when it is possible, try to connect to those who have the seeing gifts or prophetic people who can help in the process. Seers that "see" into the spirit realm can be very helpful in dealing with bloodline issues. It isn't always possible to have this available, but God will provide when it is necessary.

I see some become upset because they don't have access to these gifting. My answer is to ask the Lord to develop this in you or believe Him to bring them into your life. They are not however, a substitute for our own personal walk and seeking God. If we will set our face toward the Lord, any information we need to cleanse our bloodline, He will bring to us.

The seventh fact to help in cleansing your bloodline is to use Colossians, chapter 2, verse 14. When I use all the knowledge, both naturally and supernaturally that I have, I then invoke this verdict. I ask that anything I know or do not know be washed, cleansed and forgiven by the blood. My faith in the finished works of the Cross has great power.

CHAPTER 10

THE PROPHETIC IN THE COURTS OF HEAVEN

When presenting cases in the Courts of Heaven to undo curses, we must understand the prophetic realm. When I speak of the prophetic realm, I am not just speaking about someone prophesying a, "Thus says the Lord," word. I am talking about discerning, hearing, seeing and perceiving what is going on in the spirit realm. Then being able to move in agreement with this realm.

Jesus spoke of this is John, chapter 5, verse 19.

Then Jesus answered and said to them, "Most assuredly, I say to you, the Son can do nothing of Himself, but what He sees the Father do; for whatever He does, the Son also does in like manner." (John 5:19)

Jesus "saw," then He acted from what He had "seen." The result was a manifestation of the Kingdom of God on earth. If we are to see real breakthrough in the Spirit translated into earth, we must "see" and "perceive" prophetically into the spirit realm. From this prophetic dimension we are able to operate in The Courts of Heaven.

Unless someone would think they can't do this, let me encourage you. I believe everyone has some ability to be prophetic and function in this unseen realm. I know people who have unbelievable "seeing" gifts. They see the unseen realm like most of us see the natural realm. Usually, if you trace these people's bloodline back, you will discover these giftings operated in their ancestors. They have inherited them from generations gone by. Some may have even been attached to witchcraft, but once they were redeemed, they become powerful agents for the Kingdom of God.

People with this level of gifting must learn the proper protocol of the spirit realm. Otherwise, they can "go places" they have no business going. This can open up themselves and their families to severe demonic attack. These gifts need to be mentored by seasoned seers, who know how to function in these realms.

Others of us probably have lesser gifts in these areas. Some people "see" on a lesser level. Whereas, the ones I mentioned before see in the unseen realm on a current level or what is actually presently happening in the spirit world. Others see "movies" that depict spiritual happenings. Others see pictures that represent things in the spirit. There are those who "hear" words from the Lord. There are those who "feel" and discern in the spirit. Some even "smell" things in the spirit. There are all sorts of spiritual "senses" that need to be developed. Hebrews, chapter 5, verse 14, says we are to develop these giftings we have been given.

> But solid food belongs to those who are of full age, that is, those who by reason of use have their senses exercised to discern both good and evil. (Hebrews 5:14)

Mature people have developed their giftings to a level to be able to discern prophetically both good and evil. This doesn't happen automatically. It must be done on purpose. The Apostle Paul said that we should earnestly desire the prophetic realm. In 1 Corinthians, chapter 14, verse 1, it says we should be zealous for the prophetic.

> Pursue love, and desire spiritual gifts, but especially that you may prophesy. (1 Corinthians 14:1)

We have to go after the prophetic dimension. This is why so many people "think" they can't function here. They have never made the prophetic a pursuit. We must press into the prophetic sphere and develop the giftings that are lying dormant within most people.

There are several reasons we need this prophetic dimension to operate in the Courts of Heaven. The prophetic is absolutely essential in presenting our cases in The Courts of Heaven. Isaiah, chapter 43, verse 26, tells us we put God in remembrance and state our case. This is courtroom language.

> Put Me in remembrance; Let us contend together;
> State your case, that you may be acquitted. (Isaiah 43:26)

Putting God in remembrance is prophesying from what has been written in the books of Heaven. Every person, church, business, city, state, nation, and anything else that has a Kingdom destiny has a book. The prophetic is needed to discern what is in that book. Once that is done, it is presented in the Courts as a case. This is what we see in Daniel, chapter 7, verse 10.

> A fiery stream issued And came forth from before Him. A thousand thousands ministered to Him; Ten thousand times ten thousand stood before Him. The court was seated, And the books were opened. (Daniel 7:10)

The Court of Heaven coming to session and being ready to function was connected to the books being opened. Cases are presented out of the books which contain destinies. When we are dissolving curses, we are removing everything that is standing in the way of what is in the books from being done. It is the prophetic that presents these cases. This can be done through praying prophetically, making petitions, decreeing and even prophesying. We are presenting cases in the Courts setting in motion courtroom procedures. This will allow what has been written in the books of Heaven to become reality in the earth.

Another reason for the prophetic is it agrees with Jesus' testimony. Revelation, chapter 19, verse 10, says the testimony of Jesus is the spirit of prophecy.

> And I fell at his feet to worship him. But he said to me, "See that you do not do that! I am your fellow servant, and of your brethren who have the testimony of Jesus. Worship God! For the testimony of Jesus is the spirit of prophecy." (Revelation 19:10)

When the Bible speaks of the testimony of Jesus, it doesn't say the testimony about Jesus. The testimony of Jesus is what Jesus is testifying. The word *testimony* means evidence given. So Jesus is giving evidence from His position of High Priest, Mediator and Intercessor in the Courts of Heaven. He is giving God, the Judge, every legal thing necessary for God's will to be done. The Scripture says that testimony becomes a spirit of prophecy in the mouth of the Church. This allows the Church to prophesy in agreement with Jesus' testimony. This is necessary by God's standard for verdicts to be rendered.

Deuteronomy, chapter 19, verse 15, declares God needs more than one witness to render a verdict.

> One witness shall not rise against a man concerning any iniquity or any sin that he commits; by the mouth of two or three witnesses the matter shall be established. (Deuteronomy 19:15)

Even though it is Jesus, Who is giving the testimony, corroborating witnesses are necessary. When the Church begins to prophesy in agreement with Jesus' testimony, God has the necessary witness to render verdicts. This is why we must move into new spheres of the prophetic. We are agreeing with Jesus' testimony.

A third reason we must mature and develop in the prophetic is to sense the activity in The Courts of Heaven. Hebrews, chapter 12, verses 22-24, tells us where we have been seated and sit.

> But you have come to Mount Zion and to the city of the living God, the heavenly Jerusalem, to an innumerable company of angels, to the

general assembly and church of the firstborn who are registered in heaven, to God the Judge of all, to the spirits of just men made perfect, to Jesus the Mediator of the new covenant, and to the blood of sprinkling that speaks better things than that of Abel. (Hebrews 12:22-24)

We are told that we have come to certain places and things. In my book, *Operating In The Courts Of Heaven*, I talk about these that are listed here. These are the voices that are testifying and speaking in the Courts of Heaven. It is our job to discern what they are saying prophetically and agree with them. Ephesians, chapter 2, verse 6, tells us that we are seated together with Jesus in heavenly places.

… and raised us up together, and made us sit together in the heavenly places in Christ Jesus … (Ephesians 2:6)

So we are seated or have been given a place of governmental authority in the heavenly realm. To be seated speaks of us taking our place on a Throne in the spirit realm. We are told that we are seated with Jesus on His Throne, just like He is seated with the Father on His. The prerequisite to our being seated is that we overcome. (Revelation 3:21)

When Ephesians, chapter 6, verse 2, tells us we are

seated, Hebrews, chapter 12, verses 22-24, expands on this idea. Hebrews is telling us what is there, where we are seated. It says we have "come to" all these things in the spirit realm. It is giving us some idea of where we are and have been seated in this heavenly dimension.

We have "come to" all this activity that is in this spiritual sphere. I tell people often, that the Church needs to stop trying to get places we have already come to. In other words, we accept by faith that the veil was rent (torn down), and what we didn't have access into before the Cross, we now do. We are able to prophetically tap into the activity that is in the Courts of Heaven.

There are those who would tell us that seeing angels, encountering the great cloud of witnesses and other things mentioned here is illegal. They would say this is wrong. My contention is, if we have "come to" these, then why is it wrong for us to encounter them as God deems necessary. The passion of the Lord is to join Heaven and earth together again. What is in the heavenly realm God wants to interact with the earthly realm. Ephesians, chapter 1, verse 10, tells us the passion of the Lord.

> ... that in the dispensation of the fullness of the times He might gather together in one all things in Christ, both which are in heaven and which are on earth—in Him. (Ephesians 1:10)

One of the ultimate purposes of God is to get Heaven and earth back together. As with almost everything the Lord does, He gives us a foretaste of that which is coming. We, as New Testament believers, have now "come to" all these heavenly encounters. We should desire them, long for them and expect them. These experiences in the Courts of Heaven are prophetic in nature and greatly help us to maneuver in this spiritual place.

When you read Hebrews, chapter 12, verses 22-24, carefully, you discover that what is happening there is legal in nature. This is what we have "come to." We, therefore, should expect to encounter not just the voice of the Lord, but even other activities listed in these verses. This is as much the prophetic realm as any other dimension of hearing and seeing. We need to simply be open and by faith "point" our spirit into this place of encounter.

As a result of us having "come to" this place by virtue of where we are seated, we can encounter angels, the blood speaking, Jesus the Mediator, the spirit of just men made perfect and all the others mentioned. As these are seen, encountered and witnessed, we get prophetic understanding of what is transpiring in the Courts of Heaven. This allows us to move with more clarity in this place. We must make ourselves available to the Lord to encounter this dimension through the prophetic gifting granted us.

The Lord is moving the Church and His people into new

levels of the prophetic. Our discernment is being opened in new ways. Some have been afraid to step into these places because of wrong teaching and religious ideas. Today, the Lord is taking these away and allowing us to develop our spiritual sensitivity in new areas. As we grow and mature in this, we will be able to discern activity in the spirit realm. We will be able to prophesy in agreement with Jesus' testimony. We will be able to present cases out of the books of Heaven with prophetic preciseness that will allow Heaven to rule.

Get ready, the prophetic is being released on a new level.

CHAPTER 11

NEW LEVELS OF THE PROPHETIC FOR COURTROOM FUNCTION

After Elisha received the mantle from Elijah, there was an increase of prophetic influence released. In 2 Kings, chapter 6, verses 1-2, we see the sons of the prophets, or those in training for prophetic ministry, asking to enlarge their place.

> And the sons of the prophets said to Elisha, "See now, the place where we dwell with you is too small for us. Please, let us go to the Jordan, and let every man take a beam from there, and let us make there a place where we may dwell." So he answered, "Go." (2 Kings 6:1-2)

The only reason there would be a need for an enlarged place is because numbers were increasing. Clearly, when the administration of the mantle shifted from Elijah to Elisha, there was a marked increase in prophetic activity. There were more people coming to join the "sons of the prophets" because something had shifted in the atmosphere. More people were functioning prophetically.

I believe this is happening today. People who have never prophesied are beginning to move prophetically. Those who have moved in lesser levels are increasing to greater levels of the prophetic. Those who have moved in great dimensions are moving into astonishing new levels of prophetic activity. This is what the Prophet Joel promised. Joel, chapter 2, verses 28-29, promises an outpouring of the Spirit that will result in a wholesale release of the prophetic.

> And it shall come to pass afterward That I will pour out My Spirit on all flesh; Your sons and your daughters shall prophesy, Your old men shall dream dreams, Your young men shall see visions. And also on My menservants and on My maidservants I will pour out My Spirit in those days. (Joel 2:28-29)

When he declares sons and daughters prophesying, old men dreaming and young men seeing visions, he is speaking of an unprecedented release of the prophetic. In other words, it will not be just a few hand-chosen vessels of God who will be prophesying. It will be an outpouring of a prophetic Spirit that will empower multitudes to function in the prophetic. This is what is happening today.

The operation in The Courts of Heaven is one of the places where the increase of the prophetic is most evident.

People are understanding that encounters in the Heavenly Courts in the prophetic is necessary to God's will being done. There is an awakening to this new level of the prophetic. We see a very powerful depiction of this in Revelation, chapter 10, verses 5-11. The Apostle John has a powerful encounter that opens the prophetic up to a new dimension in his life.

> The angel whom I saw standing on the sea and on the land raised up his hand to heaven and swore by Him who lives forever and ever, who created heaven and the things that are in it, the earth and the things that are in it, and the sea and the things that are in it, that there should be delay no longer, but in the days of the sounding of the seventh angel, when he is about to sound, the mystery of God would be finished, as He declared to His servants the prophets. Then the voice which I heard from heaven spoke to me again and said, "Go, take the little book which is open in the hand of the angel who stands on the sea and on the earth." So I went to the angel and said to him, "Give me the little book." And he said to me, "Take and eat it; and it will make your stomach bitter, but it will be as sweet as honey in your mouth." Then I took the little book out of the angel's hand and ate it, and it was as sweet

as honey in my mouth. But when I had eaten it, my stomach became bitter. And he said to me, "You must prophesy again about many peoples, nations, tongues, and kings." (Revelation 10:5-11)

From this encounter, John was empowered to prophesy "about" not "to" peoples, nations, tongues and kings. In other words, as we spoke earlier, his prophetic release would give testimony in the Courts. He would prophesy the destiny of nations and present cases before the Throne of Heaven. He would prophesy what was written in the books of Heaven for nations. This is necessary to unlock destinies from the Courts. Whether it is nations or individuals, destinies cannot be unlocked until they are prophesied from the books of Heaven. This is why John is being empowered to prophesy by eating this book.

There are five distinct truths to functioning in the prophetic and presenting cases in the Courts of Heaven. Remember, it is through the prophetic unction that we present cases in the Courts of Heaven to unlock destinies.

1. The first truth is that God is releasing angelic empowerment. In Zechariah, chapter 4, verses 1-2, we see an angel showing up to awaken Zechariah, who is already a functioning prophet.

Now the angel who talked with me came back and wakened me, as a man who is wakened out of his sleep. And he said to me, "What do you see?" So I said, "I am looking, and there is a lampstand of solid gold with a bowl on top of it, and on the stand seven lamps with seven pipes to the seven lamps." (Zachariah 4:1-2)

This angel came to awaken a new prophetic ability in Zechariah, so he could see on the level he needed to see. He was awakened as one who was asleep. The angel came to awaken prophetic abilities in him that were dormant. When they were awakened, he saw on a new level.

This is happening today. An angel of prophetic awakening has been sent into the Body of Christ to awaken new levels of prophetic giftings.

I was in a service in Hawaii. I was scheduled to speak on another subject. I felt as we were worshipping that I should mention this concept and idea before I ministered on the desired thing. As I was introduced, I just told about this principle of the angel awakening prophetic abilities. Suddenly, the atmosphere of the room changed. The Fear of the Lord was instantly among us. I knew this angel I was speaking of had walked into the room. I was afraid to move for fear of interrupting anything that was happening.

As I stood there, I said, "The angel is here." My friend, who leads the work, is also a prophet. He said from his seat, "I see him. He is standing right behind you." The sense in the room was awesome, and even fearful, because of the angel's presence that had come. After a few moments, I simply moved and began to impart a new level of prophetic abilities to those who were there. I knew it was a moment we could not miss. We had to move in agreement with the angel to increase us into new levels.

God is releasing this angel in the earth today. He is taking the Body of Christ into new realms of the prophetic. We must desire, pursue and move with God's angelic presence in this hour! As we do, The Lord will supernaturally help us into these next places of prophetic abilities.

2. The second truth is we must ask for the book. In Revelation, chapter 10, John asked for the book from the angel. In verses 8 and 9, the angel gives John the book in his hand.

> Then the voice which I heard from heaven
> spoke to me again and said, "Go, take the

little book which is open in the hand of the angel who stands on the sea and on the earth." So I went to the angel and said to him, "Give me the little book." And he said to me, "Take and eat it; and it will make your stomach bitter, but it will be as sweet as honey in your mouth."

John moves at the voice from Heaven that he heard. He asked for the book in the angel's hand. If we are to prophesy destinies from the books, we must take possession of the books. Even some people do not possess their own books. Just because there is a book in Heaven (Psalm 139:16) with your destiny in it, doesn't mean you have it.

Sometimes, someone in your bloodline sold your destiny out. Esau sold his destiny, birthright and blessing to Jacob for a bowl of porridge. (Genesis 25:29-34) When he did, he sold his family line as well. If someone has sold your destiny, you need to get your book back. You need to repent for the despising of what was God-ordained in your history. You can then be freed to get your book that has your destiny in it.

When someone doesn't have their book, they have no prophetic sense of their destiny. They perhaps have wandered aimlessly, trying to discern their reason for existing. The fact that they haven't yet possessed their book is manifested in their lack of purpose. Once you have your book, you are now ready to start the process of unlocking destiny.

This is also true for nations. God needs people to possess the books of nations. There can be no unlocking of destinies until books of nations are possessed. You can only possess the books you have jurisdiction for in the spirit. We each can possess the books for our families and as individuals. Books for cities, states, nations and other spheres, can only be possessed by those who have that sphere of authority.

Angels will not give books to us that are outside our jurisdiction. John was clearly an Apostle who had jurisdiction and an authority in the nations. Therefore, the angel could release this book to him. There must be those who have attained realms of jurisdiction, so books can be given to them. The nations hang in the balance, waiting on someone to get their book and prophesy their destiny in the Court of Heaven.

3. The third truth is the books must be open. Revelation, chapter 10, verse 8, says the book was opened. This is important in prophesying the destinies in the Courts.

> Then the voice which I heard from heaven
> spoke to me again and said, "Go, take the
> little book which is open in the hand of the
> angel who stands on the sea and on the earth."
> (Revelation 10:8)

This book was open. Not all books are open. The significance of the book being opened is that John was free to receive revelation from it. When books are closed and sealed, there can be no revelation from them. It is possible to have your book, but it is still closed. Daniel, chapter 12, verse 4, speaks of a book that was sealed.

> But you, Daniel, shut up the words, and seal
> the book until the time of the end; many shall
> run to and fro, and knowledge shall increase.
> (Daniel 12:4)

When a book is sealed there is no revelation or understanding that can come from it. This book was sealed because it wasn't time for it to be known. Other books are sealed because the price hasn't been paid to open them. Isaiah, chapter 29, verse 10-11, shows that when books are sealed, prophets and seers cannot prophesy. There is no revelation.

> For the LORD has poured out on you The spirit of deep sleep, And has closed your eyes, namely, the prophets; And He has covered your heads, namely, the seers. The whole vision has become to you like the words of a book that is sealed, which men deliver to one who is literate, saying, "Read this, please." And he says, "I cannot, for it is sealed." (Isaiah 29:10-11)

When books are sealed and closed, those who even have the ability to read them, can't. This is the reason some people never get a prophetic word. People cannot prophesy over someone whose book is closed. Without an open book there will be no real prophetic word. The problem is not with the prophet, the problem is the person's book is not open. We must pay the price to get our books open. Once our books are open, we, ourselves, will get prophetic revelation of our destinies. Prophets will usually only prophesy what we already know.

I see three keys to getting books opened. In Isaiah, chapter 29, verse 10-13, it shows the first of these three.

For the LORD has poured out on you The spirit of deep sleep, And has closed your eyes, namely, the prophets; And He has covered your heads, namely, the seers. The whole vision has become to you like the words of a book that is sealed, which men deliver to one who is literate, saying, "Read this, please." And he says, "I cannot, for it is sealed." Then the book is delivered to one who is illiterate, saying, "Read this, please." And he says, "I am not literate." Therefore the LORD said: "Inasmuch as these people draw near with their mouths And honor Me with their lips, But have removed their hearts far from Me, And their fear toward Me is taught by the commandment of men ..." (Isaiah 29:10-13)

When we trace through this Scripture, we see the books are closed and unreadable because of false worship. The people are drawing near with their lips, but their hearts are far from Him. We must repent of false worship and truly begin to worship Him in reality with true hearts. When our hearts are full of love and passion for Him, from this worship our books will open. This is why prophetic releases so often comes out of worship. True worship opens books. Once the books are open, we can prophesy from them.

The second issue to seeing books open is timing. Revelation, chapter 22, verse 10, declares that the time is at hand; therefore, the books should not be sealed.

> And he said to me, "Do not seal the words of the prophecy of this book, for the time is at hand." (Revelation 22:10)

Some books open when it is time for them to be fulfilled. We are in some of these seasons where books that have been sealed are now opening. They are opening so they can be prophesied from and come to pass. We will see prophets speaking things that are now open and revealed from the books. The result will be a manifestation in the earth. Even in our own personal books, some things will begin to be revealed because it is time.

The third thing that opens the book is tears. Revelation, chapter 5, verses 2-5, shows John weeping and the book opening.

> Then I saw a strong angel proclaiming with a loud voice, "Who is worthy to open the scroll and to loose its seals?" And no one

in heaven or on the earth or under the earth was able to open the scroll, or to look at it. So I wept much, because no one was found worthy to open and read the scroll, or to look at it. But one of the elders said to me, "Do not weep. Behold, the Lion of the tribe of Judah, the Root of David, has prevailed to open the scroll and to loose its seven seals." (Revelation 5:2-5)

John wept because he knew without the book being opened and what was in it being released, God's will and passion would not be done. We must know that it is our tears of intercession that opens books. We must weep for our own destinies. We also need intercessors to weep for the destinies of nations. Without the tears of intercessions, books will not open, prophecies will not be spoken, decisions from the court will not be rendered and destinies will be lost. We must have intercessors to weep and travail until the books of Heaven, which contain the destinies of nations open. Then, what is written in these books can be presented in the Courts of Heaven and destinies unlocked!

4. The fourth truth concerning prophetically presenting cases in the Courts is it is sweet in the mouth of those

who declare it. Revelation, chapter 10, verses 9-10, show the sweetness of the word as the book was eaten.

> So I went to the angel and said to him, "Give me the little book." And he said to me, "Take and eat it; and it will make your stomach bitter, but it will be as sweet as honey in your mouth." Then I took the little book out of the angel's hand and ate it, and it was as sweet as honey in my mouth. But when I had eaten it, my stomach became bitter. (Revelation 10:9-10)

The sweetness in the mouth means the Word of the Lord toward nations is a good word. When John ate the book, the word was sweet. God's destiny over nations and even individuals is always a good word. He is not speaking judgment; He is speaking life.

What we prophesy is very important. Ten spies prophesying the wrong thing caused a whole nation to wander for forty years. Think about this. When they gave the wrong testimony about the land of Canaan, a judgment on the basis of their testimony was rendered against a nation. They prophesied the wrong word from a wrong spirit and got a wrong verdict. (Numbers 14:33-34)

We must be careful what we prophesy. When we are prophesying from the books of Heaven, we are declaring the good word of God. This is why it is sweet in the mouth. We are reminding God, as Judge, what He wrote in the books of Heaven. We are presenting our case, based on the goodness of His word.

5. The final truth about prophetically presenting a case in the Courts is it made his stomach bitter. Revelation, chapter 10, verse 9, says what was sweet in the mouth became bitter in the stomach.

> So I went to the angel and said to him, "Give me the little book." And he said to me, "Take and eat it; and it will make your stomach bitter, but it will be as sweet as honey in your mouth." (Revelation 10:9)

When something becomes bitter in the stomach it means you are nauseated. This usually proceeds vomiting. This is the picture being painted here. The word that is sweet creates such an unction in the spirit, that it cannot be contained. The idea of vomiting is a picture of the unction flowing out of our spirit as we prophesy. Amos, chapter 3, verse 8, shows the power of this unction.

A lion has roared! Who will not fear? The Lord
GOD has spoken! Who can but prophesy?
(Amos 3:8)

The Word of the Lord when eaten will create such an
unction that we cannot help but prophesy. We will spew
forth the Word of the Lord from our inner-most being,
full of the life and power of the Lord. This word released
in that power will be spoken from the book that has been
eaten. We will prophesy from the destiny written in a
book before time began. We are then presenting a case
in the Courts of Heaven. This will begin the process of
unlocking destinies from the Court of Heaven.

God is bringing us into new levels of the prophetic.
This is necessary to present cases, maneuver in the
Courts, agree with Jesus' testimony and see destinies
unlocked on every level. Exciting days are ahead, as
things are moved in the spirit realm for God's plan to
unfold in us and through us.

CHAPTER 12

STRATEGIES AND PROTOCOLS FOR UNLOCKING DESTINIES FROM THE COURTS OF HEAVEN

As we finish this book on unlocking destiny and dissolving curses, I want to be as practical as possible. The truths I have outlined in this book are secrets for breakthrough. I can say this because I not only see it in the Scriptures, but I have also experienced it in my own life. These principles and truths have changed my life.

This book is about principles that are for both individuals and families, but it is also for cities, states and nations. I believe God wants to lift curses off of every sphere of society and see His Kingdom revealed in the earth. The whole earth will be filled with the knowledge of His glory (Habakkuk 2:14) and the kingdoms of this world will become the Kingdoms of our Lord and His Christ (Revelation 11:15).

In this chapter I am going to try to be as methodical as I can. I realize that only the Holy Spirit can teach us to pray. We must follow His direction as we seek to engage the spirit realm and move into the Courts of Heaven. Romans, chapter 8, verse 26, tells us that He helps our weaknesses.

Likewise the Spirit also helps in our weaknesses. For we do not know what we should pray for as we ought, but the Spirit Himself makes intercession for us with groanings which cannot be uttered. (Romans 8:26)

The Lord realizes our limitations, as we seek to step into this world of the Courts. It pleases the Lord greatly that by faith we go here and attempt to function. Our trust and confidence that He will undergird us and secure us, as we endeavor to approach Him stirs His heart toward us. So do not allow any sense of insufficiency hinder or stop you. Go ahead and go for it, and learn as the Spirit teaches you.

As we approach the Courts of Heaven to unlock our destiny and dissolve any curse that is set to hinder it, we must use the proper protocol. Remember, we approach God in three realms.

1.   We approach Him as Father (Luke 11:2).
2.   We approach Him as Friend (Luke 11:5-8).
3.   We approach Him as Judge (Luke 18:1-8).

This is all in my book, *Operating In The Courts Of Heaven.* When we come before Him as Father, there is no real protocol. He is your Abba Father, and He receives you. When we approach Him as Friend, there is no necessary protocol. Real friends do not need protocol to relate. But when you come before Him as Judge, there is protocol in His Judicial system.

Every Court has a realm of behavior and procedure that must be abided by. We must learn that protocol and walk in it, and allow it to govern us as we function in the Courts of Heaven.

As we approach the Lord as Judge, we should ask for the Courts to open. I use to think this wasn't necessary. I have since learned that it is. There is a Fear of the Lord associated with coming into His Courts. Not a fear of us being judged, but a Fear of the Lord that He is the Great King. We must honor Him as such.

When we come into a natural courtroom there is seriousness about the place. We wear certain clothing, and we act a certain way. This is because we recognize the weightiness of where we are. How much more the Courts of Heaven. I have found it is helpful to honor the Lord as the Judge of all to ask the Courts to open and us to be granted entrance. It is very much like Esther waiting on the king to extend his scepter and invite her into his courts. Esther, chapter 5, verse 2, shows this happening.

> So it was, when the king saw Queen Esther standing in the court, that she found favor in his sight, and the king held out to Esther the golden scepter that was in his hand. Then Esther went near and touched the top of the scepter. (Esther 5:2)

She waited until she was invited into the courts of the king. As we approach the Courts of Heaven in humility and yet boldness, The Judge of All will open His Courts and invite us in.

One of the things I have been doing, as I teach on The Courts of Heaven, is asking the Lord to "open the Courts" so we can just look. As I train those with the seeing gifts to see into the Courts of Heaven, this is good practice. I ask the Lord to let us come in and just look, but not function. It is amazing what the seers see, as we walk through this exercise. The purpose for it is to get people acquainted with the Courts of Heaven. When this happens, we are then getting ready to approach the Courts and present cases.

Once we are in The Courts, we can prophetically present our case. This is based on what is written in the books of Heaven about our destinies. We, through prophetic praying, prophetic decrees and prophetic petitions, state what is in our books. Perhaps it is something you know by revelation about your destiny. It can be prophetic words that have been spoke over you that you know are in the books. This is putting God in remembrance, according to Isaiah, chapter 43, verse 26.

Put Me in remembrance; Let us contend together; State your case, that you may be acquitted. (Isaiah 43:26)

This is the way we begin to deal with whatever is God's destiny for our lives. For me, I have several significant prophetic words. I have words that God has spoken to me in dreams. I have words spoken into my own spirit. I also have prophecies given to me. For example, from as far back as 35 years ago, God has spoken that I was a prophet to the nations. This word has come several times. I take this not necessarily to mean my main ministry gift is that of a prophet. This is not true. I am basically apostolic.

When the term *prophet* was used, it was simply declaring I would be a spokesman for God in the nations. This has been prophesied to me; I have had dreams and heard God clearly say this. I have also heard the Lord say, "You will disciple nations." This is exciting and humbling as well. I take these words into the Courts of Heaven, because I am confident they are in my book. I asked for all that had been pre-ordained for me to become a reality.

One of the chief means of presenting our case for our destiny in the Courts is to bring it on the basis of His Purpose and not our need. This is a critical piece to know in getting answers from the Courts of Heaven. Sometimes, I watch shows on TV about true criminal cases. They are usually about murder and who did it. In one of the shows, a husband was accused of murdering his wife. He went to trial with the District Attorney of this particular county, seeking to get a conviction. The DA presented the case and the man's legal defense team defended him. The result was a "hung jury."

This is a jury that is divided and fails to reach a verdict. When this happens one of two things occurs. Either the State drops the case against the defendant and he is free, or they can bring him back to trial again. In this instance, the man was rescheduled for another trial. In between the ending of the first trial and the beginning of the second, a new District Attorney took office. This DA completely redid the case.

She took the same facts and evidence, but presented it in a completely new way. The result was a verdict convicting the man of the murder of his wife. He was sentenced to a lengthy prison sentence. The difference in the trials was the WAY the case was presented. The same facts and the same evidence presented in a different way allowed the rendering of a different verdict.

This is true in The Courts Of Heaven. How we present our cases for destiny is critical. I have learned and am learning to present my case on the basis of His Purpose and not my need. The way I began to understand this was because of a prayer situation I found myself involved in. There is a very high-ranking State official who I was asked to pray for. He was under indictment for supposed criminal activity. If convicted, he would lose everything and go to prison for a very long time. His family would be completely decimated and destroyed as well. The problem was, he was completely innocent. These were all politically motivated charges against a man of impeccable character. The reason he was targeted was because of his stand for righteousness in his State.

I was asked to pray with His wife and him and take this case before the Courts of Heaven. As we began to pray, I was leading this man and his wife through entrance into the Courts. We were asking the Lord to move and stop these atrocities against him. We were letting it be known that this was unrighteous and would harm this one God loved greatly. We were asking that the Lord would not allow this destruction to come to this righteous man. We asked that God would move and meet his needs in this situation.

Sounds right doesn't it? It seems like there's nothing wrong with this kind of prayer. God didn't agree. As I was leading them through this prayer, I suddenly heard the Lord loud and clear. He said to me, "Do not bring this man's case to me on the basis of his need. Bring His case to me on the basis of My Purpose in him." Wow! As the Lord said this to me, my mind began to whirl. I remembered how Moses interceded for Israel when God was going to destroy them. Exodus, chapter 32, verses 10-14, shows Moses presented his case before God on behalf of Israel.

> Now therefore, let Me alone, that My wrath may burn hot against them and I may consume them. And I will make of you a great nation. Then Moses pleaded with the LORD his God, and said: "LORD, why does Your wrath burn hot

against Your people whom You have brought out of the land of Egypt with great power and with a mighty hand? Why should the Egyptians speak, and say, 'He brought them out to harm them, to kill them in the mountains, and to consume them from the face of the earth?' Turn from Your fierce wrath, and relent from this harm to Your people. Remember Abraham, Isaac, and Israel, Your servants, to whom You swore by Your own self, and said to them, 'I will multiply your descendants as the stars of heaven; and all this land that I have spoken of I give to your descendants, and they shall inherit it forever.'" So the LORD relented from the harm which He said He would do to His people. (Exodus 32:10-14)

Moses, in no place in this Scripture, presents Israel's need to God. He makes his appeal in the Courts of Heaven based on three things.

1. He appeals to God on the basis of His purpose in Israel. Moses reminds God that they are His people. This implies your purposes in the earth are locked up in them. If you destroy them, you destroy your purposes with them.

2. The second thing he appeals to God for is His reputation. He lets God know that people will say that He only brought them out to destroy them and do them harm. His reputation and Name would be ruined in the earth.

3. Third, he reminds God of the covenant and promises He made to Abraham, Isaac and Israel. He pulled the covenant card out. He appealed to God on the basis of His character and integrity.

These are the three things Moses used to present his case before God. He did not mention need or even ask for mercy. He simply pointed out to God that if he destroyed this nation in His anger, He would be the One Who would suffer. On the basis of this courtroom activity by Moses, God relented and spared Israel.

We must learn how to present our cases on the basis of His Purpose, His Reputation and Name and His Covenant-Keeping Nature. We must stop whining to God about our need and start appealing to God about His interest in the matter. When we do, verdicts can and will be rendered on our behalf.

The reason we want our destiny is not so we can be happy. We want our destiny for His purpose to be done in the earth. This is the basis of presenting our case in the Court of Heaven! We should come before His Court and remind Him of what is written in our book that is connected to His purpose in the earth. This is the right way of presenting our case before The Lord.

Once the request and prophetic declaration has been made, the accuser will usually rise to bring his case against you. It will be connected to your sin, transgression and iniquity, or perhaps the accusations others are making against you. If there is no case presented you should ask that the accuser be made to bring anything against you to light. He loves to hide things and use things in secret. You must force him to bring his accusations into Court.

Even in the American court, there is something called "discovery." One side must show the other side the evidence they have. They are made to manifest whatever they would use against someone. In the Courts of Heaven we should demand "discovery." We want to see whatever the accuser is using to resist the destiny and even cause curses to land.

My wife Mary was suffering with a sickness that was getting worse and worse. We prayed and could not break it. We then took it into Court. To our amazement, a well-known prophet was in Court speaking against her. As we listened, we could not hear the accusation that this prophet was bringing.

Suddenly, I remembered an occasion with this prophet. This prophet had an attitude toward my wife. It was as if they were upset because I wasn't allowing my wife to be the woman of God she should be (which wasn't true). There seemed to be something as well about Mary not moving into her destiny also.

We knew this prophet's word before the Courts of Heaven were being used as an accusation against Mary. We all need to be careful with our words of criticisms.

Those who carry spiritual authority in God need to especially be careful. Our careless words and attitudes can give legal reason for curses to land. We had to deal with this accusation and repent where we needed and make decrees where we needed. When we did, the sickness was broken and Mary recovered. We must listen and discern, when in the Courts of Heaven, for what the case is against us. It can give the enemy legal rights to bring curses.

Once the legal accusations are removed, then there must be a speaking off of any curse that is there because of them. Isaiah, chapter 54, verse 17, tells us to condemn tongues against us.

> "No weapon formed against you shall prosper,
> And every tongue which rises against you
> in judgment You shall condemn. This is the
> heritage of the servants of the LORD, And their
> righteousness is from Me," Says the LORD.
> (Isaiah 54:17)

This point was mentioned earlier in the book, but the tongue is what is speaking against us in The Courts. From our position of righteousness, granted by the blood of Jesus, we speak off and condemn every curse that is trying to cling to us. *Condemn* is the Hebrew word *rasha*, and it means to do or declare wrong. It also means to disturb or violate. When we declare the judgments that have allowed curses to be wrong, we violate and interrupt them from operating.

Our righteous position in the Courts of Heaven and our heritage or birthright as His servants gives us the necessary place to dissolve the judgments that are allowing curses. We should continue to speak and remove these spiritual forces until they are completely annulled. Mark, chapter 11, verse 23, tells us to speak to the mountain until it is moved.

> "For assuredly, I say to you, whoever says to this mountain, 'Be removed and be cast into the sea,' and does not doubt in his heart, but believes that those things he says will be done, he will have whatever he says." (Mark 11:23)

We should believe the spiritual position we have been granted. From this position, we aggressively refuse to allow any negative, spiritual force to fashion our destiny. We remove every legal right of it to operate from our bloodline and any other source. Then we command it to go until every aspect of the curse is no longer operating. This is our heritage as the servants of the Lord, to live in absolute victory and destiny.

The last thing I will mention to practically come into destiny from the Courts of Heaven is to walk out the process, knowing things have been arranged in the spirit. Luke, chapter 22, verses 31-32, shows that Jesus dealt with Peter and his destiny in the Courts of Heaven. Yet, Peter was going to go through a natural process to enter into all that had already been arranged for him in the spirit.

> And the Lord said, "Simon, Simon! Indeed, Satan has asked for you, that he may sift you as wheat. But I have prayed for you, that your faith should not fail; and when you have returned to Me, strengthen your brethren." (Luke 22:31-32)

Peter was going to deny Jesus, be in hiding with the rest of the disciples, return to fishing, struggle with loving Jesus and basically question everything about himself. Yet, because Jesus had gotten things arranged in the Courts of Heaven, Peter's destiny was sure.

Just because things have been won in the Courts doesn't mean there will not be a struggle to move into it. It just means the victory and walking out the destiny is sure. We also see this in Romans, chapter 8, verses 26-28. We like to quote verse 28 about everything working together for good. This only happens if we have arranged things legally in the spirit realm through prayer.

Likewise the Spirit also helps in our weaknesses. For we do not know what we should pray for as we ought, but the Spirit Himself makes intercession for us with groanings which cannot be uttered. Now He who searches the hearts knows what the mind of the Spirit is, because He makes intercession for the saints according to the will of God. And we know that all things work together for good to those who love God, to those who are the called according to His purpose. (Romans 8:26-28)

Prayer by the Spirit and through the Spirit is what arranges everything to work together for good. Everything working for good for us is not a result of the sovereignty of God. It is the result of us going into The Courts of Heaven and seeing things arranged for our destiny and His purpose. When we do this, what has occurred in the Spirit will manifest in the natural. This is what happened to Peter and will happen also for us.

Sometimes it occurs quickly. At other times it may take a period for it to flesh out. When we deal with spiritual realities and legalities in the Courts of Heaven, our destinies will be unlocked.

We are then ready to live out the fullness intended for us in the books of Heaven. His purposes are accomplished in our lives to His glory.

Let's go to Court!

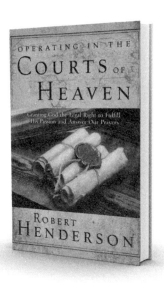

Why do some people pray in agreement with God's will, heart and timing, yet the desired answers do not come? Why would God not respond when we pray from the earnestness of our hearts? What is the problem, or better yet, what is the solution?

I believe the answer is found in where our prayer actually takes place. We must direct our prayer towards the Courtrooms of Heaven and not only the battlefield. I believe that it is in the Courtrooms of Heaven where our breakthroughs can be found. When we learn to operate there we will see our answers unlocked and released.

This book will teach you the legal processes of Heaven and your place in it. When we get off the battlefield and into the courtroom we can grant God the legal right to fulfill His passion and answer our prayers.

More great resources from

Robert Henderson

Voice of Reformation

My definition of reformation is the tangible expression of the Kingdom of God in society. One of the greatest challenges facing the Body of Christ is producing the reformers that are necessary to see these mountains re-claimed. When vision is created—intercessors are empowered and reformers are produced and commissioned into their function in these mountains—we will see a living demonstration of the Kingdom of God in Planet Earth through reformation.

The Caused Blessing

When we function in firstfruits, our influence is felt for generations to come, especially throughout our lineage. I always say that if a man's influence only lasts for the span of his natural life, then he is a failure. God intends for our influence to far outlive our natural days. One way this occurs is through the act of firstfruits.

Consecrated Business

Through the principal of firstfruits, businesses can become Kingdom in nature because they are consecrated to the Lord and become holy unto Him. This book will teach you how to birth a Kingdom Business and propel you into a new level of prosperity and influence.